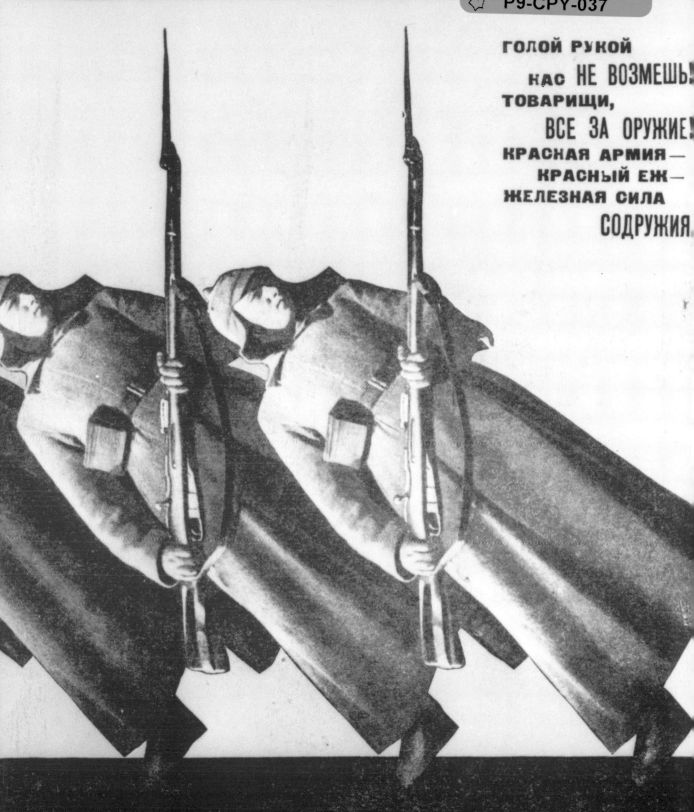

ГОЛОЙ РУКОЙ
нас НЕ ВОЗМЕШЬ!
ТОВАРИЩИ,
ВСЕ ЗА ОРУЖИЕ!
КРАСНАЯ АРМИЯ—
КРАСНЫЙ ЕЖ—
ЖЕЛЕЗНАЯ СИЛА
СОДРУЖИЯ.

Russian Avant-Garde Books   1917-34

Susan Compton

Russian Avant-Garde Books   1917-34

The MIT Press   Cambridge, Massachusetts

Endpapers
V. Mayakovsky, *Menacing Laughter*, 1932, endpapers
by V. Stepanova (C.127.d.21)

Frontispiece
Reality. Verses, 1919, cover
by A. Lentulov (Cup.403.w.19)

First MIT Press edition, 1993
© 1992 The British Library Board

Printed and bound in Great Britain.

Library of Congress Cataloging-in-Publication Data
Compton, Susan P.
    Russian avant-garde books, 1917-34 / Susan Compton. — 1st MIT
Press ed.
        p.   cm.
    Includes bibliographical references and index.
    ISBN 0-262-03201-5
    1. Book design—Soviet Union—History—20th century.
2. Illustration of books—20th century—Soviet Union.   3. Printing—
Soviet Union—History—20th century.   4. Avant-garde (Aesthetics)—
Soviet Union.   I. Title.
Z116.A3C72   1993
686—dc20   92-22918
                                                  CIP

Contents

Preface

In the years following the October Revolution hearts thrilled to the slogan 'Workers of the world unite', as workers raised their red flags in celebration of the coming of socialism. They would own the means of production forever; they would be rid of capitalism with its evils of exploitation and inequality; there would be literacy for all; paradise would come on earth [*see* cover]. Poets, painters, actors and architects, too, greeted the new era – using the latest inventions at their command. Lenin recognized the usefulness not only of printing but of film and theatre as media for propaganda: education for all was as important as electrification.

Many believed that the October Revolution would usher in a new age as, with support from the state, artists and writers published books and journals, drew posters, made newsreels and put on plays; they even built new street furniture – kiosks for disseminating information by public broadcasting. Everything was urgently discussed; the 1920s were years of intense, utopian debate. All too soon a new generation was pressing for speedier change towards socialism and pushing aside the early enthusiasts because it considered their aims and methods too idealistic. Even before Lenin's untimely death in 1924, the shadow of Stalin fell across the leadership; when Stalin strode ahead with the Five Year Plan at the end of the decade, he empowered a bureaucracy as repressive as any from Russia's past. Those who dared to remonstrate were silenced – sometimes by means of mock trials, sometimes by deportation. Before the end of the 1930s a ferocious tyranny stalked through the Soviet Union. In the years of terror of the midnight knock on the door and of the failure of justice, the optimism of the 1920s was described as a 'left-wing conspiracy' to be removed from official histories, from museums and even from libraries. In all of the arts, experimentation was buried under a tumulus of Socialist Realism which, in 1934, was sanctioned as the official artistic creed.

Today the Utopian ideas of the 1920s and the radical ways in which they were expressed are being re-evaluated. It was never possible for them to vanish because they had been recorded in contemporary journals and books, including many whose covers are reproduced here. Many found their way overseas and reached libraries such as the British Library to form a framework for study by historians. Indeed, by the end of the 1920s, Western literary scholars were well aware of the bitter arguments among writers within the Soviet Union;

'LEF'
Left Front of Art, imprint by A. Rodchenko in S. Tretiakov, *Altogether. Verses*, 1924 (11588.h.27).

7

they provided the basis of now-forgotten books quoted here. Well into the 1930s architectural journals provided a platform for the exchange of ideas between Western Europe and the USSR; later on, within the Soviet Union itself, individuals risked their lives to preserve the artefacts of those times. Paradoxically, Stalin enabled much avant-garde literature and graphic design to be kept safely, when, in 1935, he declared Vladimir Mayakovsky to be the most talented Soviet poet and 'indifference to his memory a crime'.

Most of the material illustrated and written about in these pages is to be found in London at the British Library, as was the material in the previous volume, *The World Backwards, Russian Futurist Books 1912-16*, published in 1978. Whereas the Futurist material in the British Library collection was generally acquired in recent years, many of the publications discussed here entered the Library soon after they came out. They were acquired for their texts; so, when in the course of time some of them had to undergo conservation, the first consideration was not always their artistic interest. Fortunately the standard method of re-binding meant that covers were bound in at the back of the volume, so most of them have been preserved. Although this book does not set out to be a catalogue, the British Library reference number to publications in the collection is given in the notes and captions. References to illustrations are given in square brackets.

I would like to thank all those who have helped me with this work, especially Michael McLaren Turner and Dr Christine Thomas, whose enthusiasm has resulted in the growth of the Library collection to its present eminent position.

Note on transliteration

Since the publication of *The World Backwards*, the British Library has adopted the Library of Congress system of transliteration which is used here. Modifications in the text include the use of a final 'y' in proper names to replace the strict transliteration 'ii' of the Russian original, *eg* Kandinsky instead of Kandinskii, as well as dropping the soft sign in the middle of a well-known name, thus Melnikov instead of Mel'nikov. Customary variations in names – such as El Lissitzky instead of Lisitskii and Meyerhold instead of Meierkhol'd – have also been used. The Library of Congress system has been followed throughout the notes.

The 1920s and 1930s: an introduction

Six years after the October Revolution – on Sunday 29 November 1923 – a poetry reading was held in Moscow at the Politechnical Museum under the slogan, 'Poetry of our Day'. Printed on the poster were the names of no less than seventy-one poets, grouped under various labels which were familiar to anyone who had followed the fortunes of poetry in twentieth-century Russia: Symbolists came first, then Acmeists and Futurists. In addition there were newer names, the Left Front of Arts (*LEF*) and Constructivists, Imaginists, Neo-Classicists, Neo-Romantics, Moscow Parnassus, Nothingists and Cosmists. Even these were not enough to group all the writers, for there was the additional vague heading, 'other groups and no group' – the last comprising the greatest number of names.[1] No matter that most of the labels included only two or three names, that only a handful of them are still famous, it is the clamour of poetic fervour in post-Revolutionary Russia that is so remarkable. Yet poetry was only one side of literary activity which included plays and film-scripts as well as prose of many genres – amongst them manifestos and criticism of art and architecture. The variety and complexity of writing and its transcription into printed books of striking appearance characterizes the period from 1917-34.

These years comprise the greatest inventiveness in book design; they are also years when creation in all fields, including the arts, enshrined the hope for a better life in a country which, compared to the United States and Western Europe, remained backward in spite of modernization at the beginning of the century. The 1917 Revolutions induced an atmosphere of general excitement at the prospect of social as well as political change. The means of production were to belong to the workers, as the capitalist system was dismantled. The right to divorce was welcomed, as marriage laws had been exceptionally archaic in Tsarist Russia, where no one in the military or civil service could marry without the permission of their superiors, and the obedience of married women to their husbands was enshrined in the legal code.[2] Creative minds expected the overthrow of the Tsar to lead to greater democratization and the new technology to usher in an ordered and productive world, where society would be free from religious taboos and men and women would gain new freedom from the constraints of family life. The family as a unit was expected to become redundant as women asserted their equality as workers and left the home, with its ties of child-bearing and rearing. Workers would choose to live a collective life, sharing

1
V. Mayakovsky, ed. by
V. Katanian, 1931, cover
with poster by
Mayakovsky (C.135.g.8).

facilities for eating, child-minding and leisure. Already in 1918 blocks of apartments built as investments for rental were nationalized and renamed Housing Communes; the occupants organized themselves into voluntary associations with rules to regulate the lives of the members, who, until 1921, paid no rent. By the end of that year over eight hundred housing communes were registered in Moscow, though communal ways were slow to catch on and architects, amongst others, thought the system could be speeded up if structures were purpose-built. Theories of collectivization met with approval in all areas of thought, for collectivization would bring about the brotherhood of man.

Avant-garde writers and artists – including architects – led the way with Utopian ideas. Some objectives were straightforward, such as the achievement of universal literacy; this was seen as an imperative in a country where the greater proportion of the population could neither read nor write. Just after the second anniversary of the Revolution it became compulsory for all illiterates between the ages of eight and fifty to learn to read and write, though the task took years to implement, let alone achieve success. Statistics illustrate the problem – more than fifty million adults became literate in the twenty years from 1920 to 1940.[3] Part of the reason for the remarkable-looking books of the 1920s was the designers' enthusiasm for encouraging reading by making printed matter look inviting to a wide range of tastes [1]. As well as the book covers – which often look like advertisements for the contents – reading matter was advertised[4] and books published by the State were soon available for purchase on street corners in specially designed kiosks where the sellers wore caps bearing the inscription 'State Publishing House'.[5] A pamphlet recording a novel initiative for making books more popular was published in 1924. Its title announces the method: *An Evening of the Book in Youth Clubs (An Experiment in Mass Artistic Agitation for the Book) (Vecher knigi)*.[6] The designer, Varvara Stepanova, constructed an over-size 'book' from screens fanned out like pages, each side decorated with enlargements of book covers. The principal character from each story was played by an actor in appropriate costume who stood between the pages and then 'came to life' in a scene in which pre-Revolutionary 'baddies' were vanquished by post-Revolutionary 'goodies'. The designs were witty and the evening enlivened by clowns and a chorus-line. With their uniform height, bobbed hair, bare legs, black ankle socks and ballet shoes, and wearing Stepanova's all-in-one sports' outfits, the girls were the antithesis of a pre-Revolutionary chorus line, with a new, healthy, down-to-earth style suited to the comradeship of the times.[7] The performance was carefully rehearsed by a director, with actors using simple props; it was repeated several times for Red Army and workers' organizations.

Universal literacy was clearly a reasonable objective, but when architects predetermined a particular life-style for workers by the designs they made for collective housing, or theatre producers propagandized a social message by the plays they chose to put on, their aims could be criticized as manipulative. In the 1920s there was plenty of discussion and extreme ideas were attacked, though none of the avant-garde 'improvements' was carried out from less than the purest motives. Towards the end of the decade idealism came to be considered more and more a 'leftist' deviation. Artists and writers who had struggled to bring about a golden age now found a different kind of society thrust upon them, one which increasingly lacked freedom of expression. From 1929, when the First Five Year Plan was initiated, the common good seemed to give way more and more to the production quota, and privilege became the reward of

conformity. In the 1930s an insidious uniformity began to invade typesetting – reduced to banality, photographs – heavily retouched, or painting, sculpture and architecture – enshrined in traditional styles masquerading as 'Socialist Realism'.

Book design was at its most inventive in the 1920s, when publications were produced with visual presentation which surpassed that of most pre-Revolutionary publications except those of the Russian Futurists. For four years from 1912 to 1916 Futurist artists and writers broke with the tradition of carefully designed and finely printed books which characterized the publications of Russian symbolist writers and the World of Art group (*Mir iskusstva*). Determined to 'Throw Pushkin … overboard'[8] they developed a new way with words, attempting to break them free from layers of meaning accrued over time. To match these onslaughts on language – exemplified in trans-sense (*zaum*) poems composed of made-up words – they needed a new look for their publications so, as well as using typesetting, they experimented with unusual techniques. They duplicated handwriting and drawings by transfer lithography – a method which allowed them to produce copies the right way round for reading, but preserved the vitality of conventional lithography; they used rubber-stamped letters and typewriting on printed wallpaper and squared and lined exercise-book paper; and when they used typography for theoretical texts or poems, it was printed on cheap plain paper. These methods were suitable only for small editions of two or three hundred copies and artists further individualized some copies by colouring them by hand and by embellishing them with collage.[9] In contrast, after 1917 a much wider spectrum of publications had innovative printed covers designed by imaginative artists. The covers may be purely typographical; they may include photomontage [plate 1]; rarely, they may be created from drawings or paintings; all convey a vitality which, for over a decade, found little to equal it outside the Soviet Union. The covers of Russian books and periodicals rivalled the arresting poster designs produced in the same years, often by the same artists.

This revolution in graphic design is sometimes seen in aesthetic terms, as the product of artists alone, with scant reference to its background outside the art world. Little mention is made of the transitional period immediately after 1917, when a gradual change-over from hand-done techniques to mechanical processes took place; not much attention is given to the artists' collaborators whose writing contributed the reason for these notable designs. The work of these writers, photographers, film-makers, theatre producers and architects is usually discussed in individual studies of literature, cinema, theatre and architecture, where book design is often ignored. If cover designs are reproduced, no account is given of the literary and artistic groupings from which the publications originated. Furthermore, book design is generally seen in isolation from the political events which governed such practicalities as the availability of paper and printing facilities, or the changes in leadership and official policy which resulted in increasing government control and censorship. Finally, this area of Russian design is usually discussed as a national phenomenon, with no mention of its connections with advanced design in the rest of Europe. Of course this attempt to place avant-garde book design in its context could not have been made without recourse to the many valuable studies of aspects of the period which have enriched the literature on post-Revolutionary Russia. For over forty years it has remained a subject of fascination for writers in the West as well as in the Soviet Union.[10]

The range of original material in the British Library allows the subject to be treated in a broad manner as well as in some depth. This study deals, therefore, with books produced both by the pre-Revolutionary avant-garde in post-Revolutionary years, and with new protagonists. The poet Vladimir Mayakovsky remains the best-known avant-garde author both before and after 1917. His voice is central to the second period of the story: he roared his way through the 1920s more vociferously than the 1910s; and he played a unique role as a writer and editor. He publicly proclaimed his love for Lily Brik [see 45], wife of the theorist Osip Brik, and this connection brought him into contact with a great many writers, both political and literary, in Moscow and on his many travels throughout the Soviet Union, and as far afield as the United States and Mexico. The majority of readers know Mayakovsky's writings through one of the editions of his complete works, but the poems and plays published singly and in small collections after 1917 are evidence of his involvement with younger designers.

Mayakovsky was one of very few artists or writers to give his support to the Bolsheviks in November 1917, when the newly appointed Commissar for Enlightenment, Anatoly Lunacharsky, invited representatives from the arts to come to a meeting at the new government headquarters in Petrograd. Although welcoming the Revolution, Mayakovsky was wary of Lunacharsky, whom he described at the time as 'not the people, but "a gentleman in a jacket" from whom it is necessary to protect art, which is the property of the whole people'.[11] He avoided committing himself to work for Lunacharsky for over a year, until he joined the Visual Arts Department (*IZO*) of the People's Commissariat of Enlightenment (*Narkompros*). Unlike Mayakovsky, the theatre director, Vsevolod Meyerhold, who attended the same meeting in November 1917, worked first as head of the Theatre Department (*TEO*) in Petrograd and later, as its head in Moscow. In the early days the setting up of these new structures for the arts was often effected through personal contacts, sometimes by chance rather than by deliberate design. For example, Nikolai Punin, the art critic of the journal *Apollon*, met Lunacharsky for the first time in November 1917 when he and the composer, Artur Lourié, went to the Winter Palace to ask whether they could stage a play by Velimir Khlebnikov at the Hermitage theatre. Three years later Punin remembered how Lunacharsky:

> ... willingly and at length talked to us of art, of the tasks of the Communist Party and the position of the intelligentsia. Soon our little project of staging in the Hermitage theatre was left far behind. The question under discussion was of the organization of a new administrative apparatus in all fields of art.[12]

Following this interview, Punin joined the Petrograd *IZO* and Lourié became a member – and later, head – of the Music Department (*MUZO*) of the Commissariat. Because Lunacharsky had known him around 1913 in Paris, David Shterenberg was made head of *IZO* in Moscow and he, in turn, took on friends and colleagues to work in the department.

Before 1917, groupings within the avant-garde can conveniently be classified according to exhibiting societies, such as the Union of Youth, the Target and Hylaea, but such affiliations provide a less useful structure for the story of publications in the following years. In the 1920s, new exhibiting societies were founded but members of the Society of Young Artists (*OBMOKhU*), the Society of Easel Painters (*OST*), and the Four Arts group (*Chetyre iskusstva*) worked only occasionally in the field of book illustration and design. On the whole such artists' organizations were peripheral to the production of books and journals, though the short-lived Makovets society – active in 1922 – published two numbers of a journal;[13] Kuzma Petrov-Vodkin [2] and Pavel Kuznetsov published attractive illustrated records of their journeys in Samarkand[14] and also helped to set up the liberal journal *Russian Art (Russkoe iskusstvo)*.[15] In two issues of 1923, this provided a record of a wide range of progressive art and design [*see* 66]. Two new art colleges provided facilities for inventive design, one in Vitebsk where in 1919-20 books were virtually handmade, and the other, the Moscow Higher State Art-Technical Studios (*VKhUTEMAS*) where excellent printing was carried out from 1922 onwards.

Many new writers and artists came to prominence in the 1920s, but members of the pre-Revolutionary avant-garde also continued to produce books. There was Aleksei Kruchenykh, who was active in Tiflis under the publishing imprint 41° and then in Moscow, in the Moscow Association of Futurists (*MAF*); Mayakovsky, who played a leading role as founder of *MAF* and then editor of *LEF*; and more names from the earlier period, Vasily Kamensky and Khlebnikov (who died in 1922), though these two took a smaller part in the literary scene than they had in the hey-day of the avant-garde movement, Russian Futurism.[16] Moreover, these writers, who now wrote prose as often as poetry, almost never worked in partnership with the same artists, for Olga Rozanova unexpectedly died in 1918; Mikhail Larionov and Nataliia Goncharova had emigrated in 1915; David Burliuk left Moscow, first for the East in spring 1918, and then for New York via Japan. Before leaving Russia, Burliuk established an outpost of Futurism in Vladivostok which contributed to the formation of *LEF*, so his exodus was to provide fresh support for the Left in Moscow in 1922. Larionov and Goncharova continued to produce books from 1919 onwards in Paris[17] as did David Burliuk in New York,[18] but connections with their homeland were slight (though Mayakovsky visited them on his travels). He brought back Larionov's cover and illustrations for the poem, *The Sun (Solntse)*[19] which was printed in Moscow in 1923. The cover, with its Dadaist arrangement of letters making up the name of the poet [3], stands out as very different from the simplified style of lettering and imagery of contemporary design in Russia [*see* 86]; this was also the case with an earlier cover, designed by Goncharova with equally inventive lettering [4], for a book by Mikhail Tsetlin published jointly in Paris and Moscow, *Transparent Shadows (Prozrachnye teni. Obrazy)*.[20] Both covers reflect the two emigré artists' personal development away from Russian Futurism while they were living in Western Europe, isolated from the changes in aesthetic approach which had taken place in Moscow in the intervening years.

In Russia, avant-garde writers teamed up with a younger generation of artists who were more politically committed to the Revolution. Some of them gave up fine art in the autumn of 1921 in favour of 'laboratory art' which they felt drew them closer to workers than artists had been before. They coined the name Constructivism for their activities, which reached into the theatre and architecture as well as graphic and industrial design.[21] Outstanding new names are those of Lazar (El) Lissitzky and Aleksandr Rodchenko, who carried out a radical reconstruction of the appearance of printed books; their role is more accurately described as designer than artist. There were other artists who played a lesser, though important role in book design: among them were Kirill Zdanevich

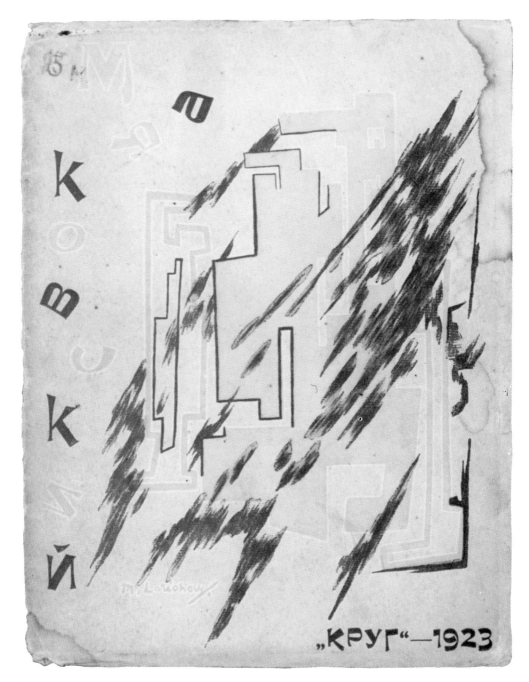

„КРУГ"—1923

3
V. Mayakovsky, *The Sun*,
1923, cover by M. Larionov
(C.114.mm.15).

4 ▷
M. Tsetlin (Amari),
Transparent Shadows, 1920,
cover by N. Goncharova
(Cup.408.i.20).

Мих. Цетлинъ
(Амари)

Прозрачныя тѣни

Парижъ

17

and his brother, Ilia (who was also a writer); the Constructivists Gustav Klutsis and Georgy Stenberg, and, later, Solomon Telingater. However, two artists who had provided art works as illustrations for poetry anthologies in the earlier period – Vladimir Tatlin and Kazimir Malevich – now furthered their activities with texts in support of Utopian artistic theories and projects: Malevich propagated his theory of Suprematism (*Ot Sezanna do suprematizma. Kriticheskii ocherk*);[22] Tatlin was soon described in a book by his supporter, Punin, as *Against Cubism (Tatlin: protiv kubizma)*.[23]

In addition, some figures whose names were less prominent in the earlier period covered in *The World Backwards: Russian Futurist Books 1912-16* must be reintroduced and reconsidered to provide an introduction to their post-Revolutionary work. For example, an artist belonging to the Knave of Diamonds group, Aristarkh Lentulov, was connected with the Hylaean group of Futurists (David Burliuk, Mayakovsky and Kamensky) before 1917 and contributed designs to several publications. One of his set designs for a proposed production of Mayakovsky's play, *Vladimir Mayakovsky. A Tragedy (Vladimir Maiakovskii. Tragediia)*,[24] was reproduced in colour in the journal *Moscow Masters (Moskovskie mastera: zhurnal iskusstv)*[25] for which he designed the cover, using hand-drawn letters in an uncluttered style. He also contributed a drawing to the miscellany, *The Archer (Strelets)*,[26] designed the cover for the anthology *Four Birds (Chetyre ptitsy)*,[27] and provided illustrations for Kamensky's novel *Stenka Razin (Sten'ka Razin)*.[28] Through his friendship with Kamensky, he was invited in 1919 to make a cover for *Reality. Verses (Iav'. Stikhi)*[29] for which he produced an elaborate topical design showing workers, factories and red flags [see front cover]. This anthology brought together a motley group of poets: as well as Kamensky, there was the Futurist sympathiser, Boris Pasternak, the Symbolist Andrei Bely, the independent 'Ruralist' Sergei Esenin, and Riurik Ivnev, Anatoly Mariengof and Vadim Shershenvich. The last three writers, joined sometimes by Esenin, styled themselves 'Imaginists' and published their own anthology [*Imazhinisty*][30] in 1925 with a cover by the Constructivist artist, Georgy Stenberg [see 27].

Another more prominent name from the years before 1917 is that of Sergei Bobrov, whose article on book design – printed in his book of poems *Gardeners over the Vines (Vertogradari nad lozami)* of 1913 – was mentioned in *The World Backwards* in connection with the illustrations made by Goncharova.[31] The importance of the same artist's cover design for Bobrov's magazine *Centrifuge*, No.2 (*Tsentrifuga*) has been noted elsewhere[32] and Bobrov continued to publish books under this imprint into the 1920s. Printing was Bobrov's hobby and he 'sabotaged' Goncharova's *Centrifuge* colophon for the covers of his collection of poems, *Lyre of Lyres (Lira lir)*[33] by partially obscuring her enlarged letter 'Ts' with random blocks of type and scribbling, and then writing the title and price by hand over the top. The covers [5] rank as an early example of adventurous printing, independent of the contemporary developments in typography in Tiflis discussed below. Bobrov was also responsible for one of the very first photomontage covers, made by Liubov Popova [plate 2] for his 1922 novel, *Revolt of the Misanthropes (Vosstanie mizantropov)*, discussed in Chapter 3.[34]

The poet Nikolai Aseev – who in the 1920s collaborated many times with Mayakovsky – had begun his career under the aegis of Bobrov, though as early as 1914 he had founded his own publishing enterprise, Liren, with another provincial, Grigory Petnikov. Aseev's 1914 collection, *Zor*,[35] with its zany cover,

5
Lyre of Lyres, 1917, cover
by S. Bobrov (Cup.408.i.15).

6
A. Kruchenykh, *The Robber
Ivan-Cain and Sonia the
Manicurist*, 1926, cover by
M. Siniakova (Cup.408.i.26).

hand-written text and illustrations by Maria Siniakova, is close in spirit to books
by the Hylaean group, as is a manifesto written by Aseev and Petnikov to
introduce their anthology, *Letorei* (an untranslatable title).[36] The two writers might
have been more closely linked to Hylaea had their journal *'Wordologist' (Slovoved)*
been published, as it was planned to include contributions from Mayakovsky,
David Burliuk, Khlebnikov and Kruchenykh, as well as Ivnev and Mikhail
Matiushin.[37] Connections were, however, cemented in the early 1920s when
Petnikov was the joint author with Khlebnikov of Kruchenykh's *Transrationalists
(Zaumniki)*,[38] and, later on, his sister-in-law, Siniakova, provided a cover [6] and
illustrations in a pre-Revolutionary, primitivistic style to Kruchenykh's detective
story, *The Robber Ivan Cain and Sonia the Manicurist (Razboinik Van'ka-Kain i Son'ka
Manikiurshchitsa)*.[39] In the 1920s Aseev and Mayakovsky produced propaganda
booklets,[40] some of whose covers are reproduced here [7 and *see* plate 4].

These groupings provide a degree of continuity between pre- and
post-Revolutionary years, but the most important change in avant-garde book
production after 1917 was its dependence on political directives, which inevitably
played an increasingly dominant role in all cultural affairs. In the previous years
historical events had – as a matter of course – impinged on the avant-garde,
especially after the outbreak of the Great War in 1914, yet political considerations
had influenced book production by Russian Futurists and related groups hardly at
all. The main constraints had been finding money for publications and gaining the
censors' approval for them once they were ready to sell. The second problem was
lifted briefly when censorship was abolished for the six months following the
February Revolution, but, three days after the Bolsheviks took power, what was
described as 'temporary' censorship was reintroduced by a decree putting a ban
on subversive organs of the Press. Early in 1918 a Commissariat of the Press was
established to administer publishing, and a Revolutionary Press Tribunal was set
up to enforce the decree.[41] Decrees on *belles-lettres* were passed soon afterwards,
nationalizing the works of the great classical writers of the past, with a directive
to the Commissariat of Enlightenment to make them available in cheap editions.[42]

Private book publishers were not outlawed straightaway, though a
State Publishing House *(Gosizdat)* was established first as a department within the
Commissariat of Enlightenment and then as an independent body in May 1919. It
was intended to do away with rivals, since the decree stated that the publishing
activities of all learned and literary societies, and likewise of all other publishing
firms *(ie* private firms) were to be subject to its regulation and control.[43] *Gosizdat*'s
power lay in its control of the means of producing printed material, as well as its
planning and sanctioning of the output of private firms. In practice, the system
was so inefficient that no author or publisher was prosecuted for illegal
publishing, and when *Gosizdat* forbade private publications a few times in 1920 it
was due to typographical shortages and scarcity of paper rather than political
disapproval.[44] The requisition of printing presses by *Gosizdat* was a hindrance to
private publishing which was further handicapped by the unreliability of those
available; presses often stopped work for weeks on end.[45] The result was that the
numbers of privately-published books dropped from nearly three hundred in
1919, to just over one hundred in 1920 and to an all-time low between January and
August 1921, when only twenty-three came out; furthermore, by 1920 the annual
output of titles had dropped to two thousand, compared with the thirty-four
thousand of 1913.[46] Periodical publishing also suffered: after an unsuccessful

А. КРУЧЕНЫХ

Разбойник ВАНЬКА-КАИН
и СОНЬКА МАНИКЮРЩИЦА

Издание Всероссийского Союза Поэтов

Москва — 1925

attempt on Lenin's life in June 1918, all independent, non-Bolshevik periodical publications were suppressed, and, a year later, all non-essential periodicals were closed down for economic reasons.

Appropriately, the years of the Civil War – which lasted from 1918 to 1920 – have been described as those of the spoken, rather than the written, word, partly because shortages limited book production so severely. Priority was given to educational books; in a pamphlet published in English in 1919, Lunacharsky told his readers that the year before, from the first '"Red Train" of Propaganda', over twenty thousand pamphlets and books were sold for ready cash in the first seven days and sixty thousand educational books were distributed freely to various local soviets; on the same page there was a description of 'Russian Railwaymen and Education': 'Along the railway line Moscow–Kiev–Voronesh [sic] the railwaymen on their own initiative have organized elementary and secondary schools. Books, teaching and meals are provided free.'[47]

Such largesse must have been a drain on limited resources and a new propaganda outlet was inaugurated in 1919 in order to reach a wider public using less paper than pamphlets and books. It was proposed that wall newspapers should be distributed throughout the country; however, the artist entrusted with the design of the first of these, Mikhail Cheremnykh, produced window posters instead, and these were issued by the Central Telegraph Agency (ROSTA; later known as TASS). Mayakovsky was the best-known contributor and the inventor of the well-known cartoon-like format [see 1]; he provided verses and, occasionally, pictures in a distinctive style owing much to the traditional marriage of word and image in folk broadsheets (lubki). He already had experience of poster design, for in Petrograd he had made propaganda posters for the Great War in the form of modern lubki and posters for Maxim Gorky's publishing house, Parus, in 1916. ROSTA posters in Moscow were duplicated by stencilling but in Petrograd some were made with linocut and some hand-painted with the lettering added separately.[48] The last method was extensively used by Vladimir Lebedev, whose posters were finely reproduced in colour in a publication [8], intended for export, as the title – Russian Placards 1917-1922 – is given only in English and French.[49]

Once peace was negotiated, the economy was bankrupt and Lenin attempted to overcome the dire conditions of everyday living through the establishment of a limited market economy. His New Economic Policy (NEP), initiated in March 1921, resulted in greater freedom for writers to publish their own material in Russia and abroad. The favourable exchange rate made Berlin the obvious place for Russians to publish books and periodicals; in the early 1920s Germany was the only country within Western Europe with which Soviet Russia had set up diplomatic and commercial relations, so many publishers – including the State Publishing House – opened branches in Berlin, where some interesting books were produced by independent Russian publishers [9]. Although in 1922 over three hundred private publishers had registered with Gosizdat in Moscow and Petrograd[50] private publishing in Russia did not increase very much in the first two years of NEP due to continuing shortages: it grew only from twenty per cent of the total in 1922 to twenty-five per cent in 1923. In the 1920s as a whole the proportions of different types of books published privately and by the State give some idea of the low government priority for literature and books on the arts: half of all books on painting, theatre and sport were privately published, compared with forty-two per cent of literary books (including poetry) and only a third of

RUSSIAN PLACARDS
PLACARD RUSSE
1917 — 1922

8
Russian Placards 1917-22,
1923, cover by V. Lebedev
with poster design by
Lebedev (C.191.a.13).

9 ▷
A. Blok, *The Twelve* [1922],
cover by V. Masiutin
(11585.l.35).

А.БЛОКЪ.

ДВѢНАДЦАТЬ

ИЗДАТЕЛЬСТВО „НЕВА" БЕРЛИНЪ

25

books on philosophy and psychology.[51] Even the State Publishing House publications were subject to restriction: according to the chief editor, each of the journals published by *Gosizdat* – which included *LEF* – was allotted exactly the same amount of paper.[52] Journals rarely ran to more than three hundred pages in a single issue and the continuous shortage of paper in Russia throughout the 1920s meant that it was often not possible for monthly journals to publish as many as twelve issues a year.

Book production was increasingly brought under Party control with the founding of a Central Administration for Literary Affairs and Publishing (*Glavlit*) in 1922. Ominously, its constitution stipulated that one of its two deputy heads was to be a representative of the security police.[53] Restrictions on publishing were matched by restrictions on the sale of books: in October 1918 a decree was issued for the municipalization of the book trade and six months later, the sale of new books ceased. Until autumn 1921 all books and printed matter were distributed free of charge by the Central Agency of the All-Russian Central Executive Committee of the Congress of Soviets (*Tsentropechat'*) and its local organs. This was in line with the prevailing system of allocation for most goods during the Civil War but the situation changed with the introduction of *NEP*. By the end of 1921 private and co-operative publishers were allowed to sell their books at market prices without government subsidy,[54] and with improved conditions new journals began publication. By then there were around thirty bookshops in Moscow as well as trade in books in the market. There was only one official Soviet bookshop, run by the Moscow Soviet; the rest were managed by writers or co-operatives.[55]

The majority of books discussed in the following chapters were produced between 1922 and 1928 and, although literature was a topic for Party discussion, comparative freedom of opinion was allowed during those years and inventiveness in appearance was unhampered. None the less, there was fierce argument between traditionalists and progressives and, in 1925, the Central Committee passed a resolution 'On Party politics in the realm of *Belles-Lettres*' (that is, on studies and writings of a purely literary kind) in an attempt to lessen quarrels between rival factions.[56] The resolution affirmed entry into a 'phase of cultural revolution'; but, although 'neutral art' was declared impossible, proletarian writers were praised and 'fellow travellers' – the name given to independent writers who had not joined the Party – defended. A Federation of Soviet Writers was formed with the intention of bringing all writers into the class struggle, yet there remained a remarkable degree of tolerance of a wide range of approaches to creative writing.

As the 1920s drew to a close publications saw the benefit of technical improvements, especially in printing. A huge All-Union Exhibition of Printing was organized in Moscow in 1927 with an adventurous catalogue [10 and *see* plate 14] designed by Lissitzky and Telingater (*Vsesoiuznaia poligraficheskaia vystavka. Putevoditel'*).[57] During the second half of the 1920s Lissitzky and Rodchenko exploited improved printing processes with numerous book covers, using photography and photomontage in creative ways [*see* 51, 53]. Soviet periodicals also benefited from better facilities: architectural journals were well-illustrated with examples of new buildings from Europe and the Soviet Union, and books by Iakov Chernikhov, presenting Utopian buildings often printed in colour, are still inspiring today. (These are discussed in Chapter 5.)

10
*All-Union Printing
Exhibition. Catalogue*, 1927,
showing the index system
designed for the book by
S. Telingater
(Cup.410.e.87).

A major change took place in 1928 when *NEP* was abolished and, in a bid for Socialism, the First Five Year Plan was ratified. When the Plan took effect in 1929 the economy was put on an increasingly war-like footing and rationing was introduced during the year: none the less, the construction of a number of new printing plants was begun and existing plants were modernized.[58] Many writers and artists adopted an almost Messianic tone in the struggle to hasten industrialization, not without the forceful encouragement of the Party in all areas, including the arts. In December 1928 the conclusions of an All-Union Conference on Agitation, Propaganda and Cultural Work, which had been held by the Central Committee the previous summer, were embodied in a resolution. This policy document became the Communist Party programme for literature for the following years.[59] It was not only directed at writing, but indicated what books publishing houses should choose and how they should select writers and give them assignments. They were instructed to favour writings of a socially useful character. The slogan 'Literature should help the Five Year Plan' was a favourite and writers and artists in search of factual material paid visits to the huge construction sites where new dams were being built to provide hydraulic power, and new railways and canals were opening up the country. Quarrels between extremists were frequent: literary and artistic groups argued that their own position was the 'correct' approach.

The 1928 resolution resulted in severe restriction of earlier more varied viewpoints. For instance, in 1923 in *LEF* No.1, Brik had defined poets and literary figures simply as experts, as good craftsmen who know how to use 'the devices of poetic craft' and had insisted that 'the social role of the poet cannot be understood by an analysis of his individual qualities and habits'.[60] His was a minority viewpoint, but when a book giving a detailed description of those 'individual qualities and habits' of writers was published in 1930 it came under fire from the censors as soon as it was published. *How We Write (Kak my pishem)*[61] – which incidentally has a respectable cover by a designer named as M. Kurnarsky [11] – set out to encourage would-be writers by giving details of how established authors worked. The contributors, who represented a range of opinions, answered questions such as, 'When do you work – morning, evening or night?' 'How many hours a day?' 'Average productivity?' 'Do you take narcotics while writing?' 'How much?' 'Do you use pencil, ink, or typewriter?' 'Do you draft a plan? To what extent do you execute it?' and other questions about their techniques and personal habits.[62] Although the traditionalist Maxim Gorky was one of those interviewed (as well as the Symbolist Andrei Bely, the theorist Viktor Shklovsky and the younger fellow travellers, Boris Pilniak, Aleksei Tolstoi, Iury Libedinsky, and Evgeny Zamiatin), the book was thought so harmful that the edition of ten thousand was withdrawn. The reason was sought by an American, Louis Fischer, who, in a book published in New York in 1932, decided that the censors' objections must have lain in what the book left out rather than in what it contained.[63] He found 'theme' to be the crucial problem for Soviet authors and identified the writers in the worst predicament to be the fellow travellers – because they were intellectuals and individualists, still writing about the past. Though still tolerated in 1925, they remained 'for' the revolution but not 'of' it and, by 1930, they were expected to decide positively one way or the other. As well as Shklovsky and Pilniak, Fischer named Marietta Shaginian (the author of *Mess Mend*, described in Chapter 3) and Isaak Babel among the fellow travellers.[64] The time for intense

Андрей Белый

М. Горький

Евг. Замятин.

Мих. Зощенко

В. Каверин

Б. Лавренев

Ю. Либединский

Ник. Никитин

Борис Пильняк

М. Слонимский

Ник. Тихонов

А. Толстой

Ю. Тынянов

Конст. Федин

Ольга Форш

А. Чапыгин

Вяч. Шишков

В. Шкловский

КАК МЫ ПИШЕМ

persecution had not yet arrived, however, for in 1932 Babel was able to publish his *Short Stories (Rasskazy)*[65] with illustrations by Shterenberg. From the outside, the book – with its hard cover of plain blue cloth stamped with a realistic motif – lacks the advertising quality of designs from the 1920s; the volume is graced by drawn illustrations [12], rather than the more avant-garde photomontage.

Such books could still be published, although the duties of *Glavlit* had been tightened the year before: in a new decree, censorship was to be carried out both before and after publication. In a second decree, extending the role of censors, *Glavlit* was given power to control manuscripts, drawings, paintings, broadcasts, lectures and exhibits to be printed, made public and disseminated, and to enforce censorship; the number identifying the local *Glavlit* representative must appear on the last page of any printed item.[66] Restrictions were extended to writers when the aims of literature were re-formulated: a resolution taken by the Central Committee of the Soviet Communist Party in 1932, 'On the restructuring of literary organizations,' described writers and artists as 'engineers of souls' and stipulated Socialist Realism as the method for their work.[67]

The term 'Socialist Realism' had its roots in discussions in the late 1920s, where realism in art was equated with materialism in philosophy and 'thus received official sanction as correct for Marxist writers.'[68] The literary historian, Edward J. Brown, has identified three kinds of realism current at the time, each with its own defect: psychological realism, he said, 'seemed to lead into the bypath of individual psychology'; objective realism sometimes revealed negative aspects of Soviet life which were thought untypical; critical realism exposed society's faults without affirming anything. Naturalism was a further alternative, but this tended to treat 'biological rather than social factors in human development.' Yet another was the 'dialectical materialist method' in realism which was supported by the Association of Proletarian Writers (*RAPP*), but this was 'both vague and doctrinaire'. The discovery of qualifying the word realism by socialist came in 1932: 'socialist' was considered a positive term, though 'dubious if applied to literature', but it was presumed that 'the meaning of "Socialist Realism" could be worked out in practice and by directive, and would, in the end, be whatever the going authority said it was'. The result of the 1932 directive was that 'literature tended to become an organized and disciplined effort whose social purposes far transcended the individual human being.'[69]

Stalin was considered to be the inventor of the term 'Socialist Realism'; this seems plausible because, unlike Lenin, he held definite views on literature. In the 1932 book already referred to, Fischer recorded that 'some time ago' a group of Communist writers had visited Stalin who reprimanded them for producing work which would be forgotten in ten years' time; he suggested that they should take Shakespeare as their model and take longer to 'do a job of more permanent value.'[70] In spite of this, Leopold Averbakh – a Party member and leading member of *RAPP* – was advising writers to spend less time on writing as, in the present situation, journalism was more important than literature. This paradox of writers themselves apparently contributing to the destruction of their potential freedom is well expressed by Fischer, who, trying to identify the reason for the censors' disapproval of *How We Write*, suggested that a 'tight-laced Bolshevik' would say:

A Soviet author should jump out of bed at the whistle of the factory siren, go through ten minutes of setting-up exercise in 'Stalinism', take a rub-down with Spirit of Lenin, breakfast on Marx and Engels, then go to the Institute of Statistics for the latest figures on the success of the Five-Year Plan, memorize the decisions of the recent Central Committee plenum and, inspired by Soviet needs and revolutionary hopes, work for six hours each day at his proletarian novel. Dreams? Sub-conscious mental life? Your material, your inspiration, the censorious Bolshevik would say, must come from observations in new peasant collectives, in the industrial giants now rising throughout the USSR, in the struggle of the working class for a better world.[71]

In 1934 the first Congress of Soviet Writers[72] enshrined Socialist Realism as a dogma and at the same time enforced it by even more punitive censorship. Censorship was to include the appearance as well as the contents of books and periodicals, so the role of the book designer was severely limited.[73] As one writer has observed, for the first time in history, censors became judges who gave the final verdict on what was, or was not, art.[74] Notwithstanding these restrictions, several artists succeeded in working within the system and from the 1930s there are occasional examples of publications with inventive designs. This is especially true of periodicals intended for overseas readers, still designed by Lissitzky and Rodchenko. But the dynamic viewpoints which had typified Rodchenko's photographs in the later 1920s – and incidentally linked them to films directed by Dziga Vertov[75] – was replaced by a more conventional and 'realist' approach. In an article on photography published in *New LEF* No.5 in 1928, Rodchenko had written:

The most interesting visual angles of our age are the bird's eye view and the worm's eye view, and we have to adopt them in our work. I do not know who discovered them, but I suppose they have been in existence for a long time. All I have to do is to improve their application and get them accepted.[76]

By 1935, when an exhibition under the title 'Masters of Photographic Art' was held in Moscow, Rodchenko had found it prudent to modify his position. His statement is so unlike his approach in the 1920s that he must surely have written it under duress:

I have stopped rebelling and trying to be original; I am no longer rash in shooting my photos; I no longer photograph in perspective for perspective's sake, nor from bird's eye view, whether it is necessary or not. I work on the contents, rather than on the appearance of the pictures.[77]

The following year he adopted a position of public self-criticism typical of these years of increasing fear. At an art debate under the slogan 'Against formalism and naturalism', he said:

It is not easy to speak when one's whole life-work is being called in question. And who should be the first to question it, but the artist himself. This is a difficult problem, painful to talk about, for one not only has to judge works that required a tremendous creative effort, but also to explain their contents, technique and method. Every piece of my work was created in the spirit of the attitude to life that I had fought for, and with every one I aimed at a high standard of technical skill.[78]

The fear and mental confusion that accompanied such an admission was only publicly recognized many years later, when some of the horror of Stalin's reign of terror – at its height from 1936 to 1939 – became known during

АПРЕЛЬ—МАЙ

19 ■ МОСКВА ■ 23

ЛЕФ

ВОСС
ТАНИЕ
МАШИН

В. АНТРОПОВ

Krushchev's term of office; the full extent of Stalin's purges was only generally admitted in the Soviet Union many years later, though books published in the West had revealed the terror of his persecutions.[79]

In a climate of enforced self-criticism and strict censorship, Soviet book covers became uniformly dull in the later 1930s, with hard covers formed from plain materials, often slightly textured, laid over cardboard. Sometimes they were embossed, and occasionally there are discoveries to be made inside the book. An example is a 1938 book about Moscow (*Moskva rekonstruiruetsia*)[80] which Rodchenko and his wife, Stepanova, illustrated with plans, photographs and statistical tables ingeniously devised and compellingly laid out. Small circular windows allow the reader to lift a portion of a view of the outside of a map or a building and see through to a view of the inside printed on the next page; statistical tables are embellished with isotypes, for example, hospital beds and taps (representing numbers of clinics and availability of running water) which are neatly drawn and coloured [13]. The whole anticipates books published twenty years later in the West. This, however, is an exception; as a rule, book design in the Soviet Union lost its world primacy after 1935.

This was the end of an era which had begun with high hopes and exuberant spirit. The 1920s had seen the development of book design from unpretentious beginnings, until, by the end of the decade, innovative designs were commonplace. Books of all shades of opinion were dressed in attractive and eye-catching printed covers – not necessarily signed by a particular designer. Comparisons between the covers of books by Sergei Tretiakov from the years 1922 to 1931[81] demonstrate the professionalism and originality which developed during that period. Although the size of the edition is not in every case recorded, the print-run of several was large by Western standards – for *Svanetia (Svanetiia)*[82] of 1928 [14], one hundred and fifty thousand, and even for the final one of the series, *Den Shi-khua: A Bio-Interview (Den Shi-khua: bio-interv'iu)*,[83] seven thousand – so books with outstanding designs like this one by Rodchenko could hardly be described as of only minority interest. The design of the contemporary *Sume Cheng the Chinese Woman (Kitaianka Sume-Cheng)*[84] also by Rodchenko may deserve the tag 'Formalist': the layout of pages of photographs and the cover [plate 3] make use of staves used by Chinese acrobats and the lettering mimics Chinese characters. Fortunately, the text is a factual account of a Chinese revolutionary, translated from the French, a subject which was surely acceptable on every count. In spite of his liberties Rodchenko escaped Stalin's purges and it was the writer, Tretiakov, who fell victim.[85] There can be few movements in the history of art which boasted such vitality and suffered so tragic an ending.

13
*The Reconstruction of
Moscow*, 1938, text by
V. Shklovsky, diagrams by
A. Rodchenko and
V. Stepanova showing the
proportion of dwellings
with running water in the
different sectors of
Moscow on 1 January 1931
(LR.274.d.30).

С. ТРЕТЬЯКОВ

№ 14

СВАНЕТИЯ

Библиотечка
„Рабочей Москвы"

ИЗДАТЕЛЬСТВО
„Рабочая Москва"
Москва, Тверская 42

14
S. Tretiakov, *Svanetia*, 1928,
designer unidentified,
printed in blue.
(010058.s.6).

2

Writers and Designers: new partnerships

Mayakovsky will be mentioned here more than any other writer, for his post-Revolutionary partnerships with artists resulted in adventurous book covers rivalling those of the previous years. Unlike the artists with whom he had worked before 1917, his new partners, such as Anton Lavinsky and Rodchenko, worked as designers rather than as fine artists, laying out pages for printing, using variations on a grid system devised by Aleksei Gan [15]. Mayakovsky also produced propaganda booklets with his poet friend, Aseev, with illustrations deliberately aimed at a barely literate public [plate 4]. On different occasions Mayakovsky brought most avant-garde writers together through the journals he edited [*see* 86]; he was active in film-making and writing scenarios; his plays (discussed in Chapter 4) attracted a great deal of attention. It is no coincidence that he committed suicide in 1930, when he foresaw the hardening of official policy towards the arts. Right up to the end he believed in the enduring continuity of his aims and he entitled his exhibition in February 1930, 'Twenty Years of Work'.[1] He included the whole range of avant-garde books with which he had been involved, from the intentionally shocking *A Slap in the Face of Public Taste (Poshchechina obshchestvennomu vkusu)* of 1912, with its sack-cloth cover,[2] to the recently published *No Admittance without Previous Announcement (Bez doklada ne vkhodit')*,[3] with its mysterious photograph filling the page [16]. He ensured the permanence of this record of his life's work by giving the entire contents of the exhibition to the State Museum of Literature immediately after the show closed, and when Stalin announced 'indifference to his memory and to his work' to be 'a crime',[4] avant-garde design was preserved, not only in its post-1917 guise discussed here, but also in its earlier phase.

Mayakovsky's loyalty to Futurism is undisputed, though the term 'Futurism' came to have a wider meaning after the October Revolution than it had had before. By 1919 the label came to be used – commonly in a pejorative way – for all radical art, whether Cubist, Suprematist, Expressionist, and after 1921, Constructivist.[5] All of these movements except the last had existed alongside Futurism before 1917, but younger artists who specialized in book-cover design were nearly all Constructivists and their work predominates in these pages. The literary branch of Constructivism will be discussed later in this chapter, while Constructivism in the visual arts – including theatre design – will be treated in more detail in the chapters devoted to those fields.

15
Contemporary Architecture, No.2, 1930, inside back cover: Rodchenko's photograph of his advertisement for books and below, diagrams by A. Gan: centre, title page of *Cinema-Photo,* No.1, 1922, right, proposal for *Time* No.1, 1924 (C.185.bb.2).

КОНСТРУКТИВИЗМ В РЕКЛАМЕ
А. М. РОДЧЕНКО

Конструктивист Родченко, организатор и руководитель металлического факультета Вхутемаса, последнее время работал в области рекламы. Им сделано несколько сот плакатов, листовок и обложек, а также несколько вывесок и ниш для магазинов Госиздата. Помещаемый рядом снимок—одна из его работ: реклама Государственного Издательства в Москве на столбе дугового фонаря. Фото А. Родченко.

КОНСТРУКТИВИЗМ
В НАБОРЕ И ВЕРСТКЕ
АЛЕКСЕИ ГАН

В полиграфическое производство конструктивизм вошел в 1922 году. До этого времени конструктивист Алексей Ган верстал ряд отдельных изданий, в которых хотя и применялись принципы конструктивизма, но не было еще установлено четкой системы набора и верстки, которая только теперь вошла и развивается в целом ряде наших крупных типографий. От трансформации текстового набора и активизации типографского материала (1918 г.), Алексей Ган перешел к планированию печатной плоскости (1921—22 г. г.). Следующим этапом работы следует считать уже типизацию как отдельных частей, так и всей печатной вещи в целом. Внизу помещены три работы Алексея Гана: макет для объявления, титульный лист и обложка, сделанная набором без шрифта.

Макет номера сделал Алексей Ган. Под его руководством набирали и верстали номер ученики школы группового ученичества типограф. „Красный Пролетарий". Четыре полосы обложки верстал тов. Крупкин. Фотогр. Н. И. Карабельщиков.

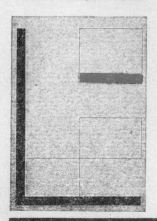

16
V. Mayakovsky, *No Admittance without Previous Announcement*, 1930, cover by S. Senkin (C.127.d.22).

17
V. Khlebnikov, *Menagerie*, 1930, cover by K. Zdanevich (Cup.408.i.39).

Mayakovsky's involvement with post-Revolutionary publications is closely rivalled by that of Kruchenykh, who had his own reasons for recognizing and perpetuating continuity with the past. In 1928 he chose the title *Fifteen Years of Russian Futurism (15 let russkogo futurizma)*[6] for his autobiography. Although he went on living in Moscow to a ripe old age (he died in 1968) this was almost the last printed book that he brought out in his role of book publisher. For two or three more years he reverted to making hand-made books – mainly cyclostyled copies of Khlebnikov's unpublished work – for distribution among that poet's friends [17], but his years as a tireless writer and impresario had come to an end. He soon reverted to teaching, living an uneventful life in a shabby Moscow apartment.[7] None the less his career is indispensable to the study of book design and his role was more central to the decade than the quality of many of his books from the 1920s would suggest.

Indeed, Kruchenykh's books provide the clearest evidence of a continuity between pre-Revolutionary Futurism and post-Revolutionary book production. He effectively avoided confronting political revolution until 1920 by staying in Georgia, a country which enjoyed a brief period of independence until 1921. In order to avoid military service he had left Petrograd late in 1915, going first to Batalpachinsk, where he taught drawing in a girls' high school. Soon he moved to Sarikamish – today in Turkey but at the time in Russian Armenia – where, in March 1916, he joined a company constructing the trans-Caucasian military railway as a draughtsman.[8] From Sarikamish he visited Tiflis and, early in 1917, with Kamensky – whom he had known in Petrograd – and the local artist, Kirill Zdanevich, prepared the books *Learn Art (Uchites' khudogi)*[9] and *1918.*[10]

In 1917 Kirill Zdanevich's brother, Ilia, also left Petrograd for Sarikamish – a town still renowned for its early Christian church architecture – where he spent the summer, presumably near Kruchenykh, before moving to his home-town, Tiflis. Previously he had been studying law in Petrograd, and he took with him the so-called University of 41°. This was apparently founded in October 1916 under the auspices of the Union of Poets, by himself and the artists Nikolai Lapshin, Mikhail Le-Dantiu, Vera Ermolaeva and Olga Liashkova. In the capital they had published a cyclostyled journal, *Murder without Bloodshed (Ubiistvo bez krovi)*, as well as holding seminars on the theory of modern poetry.[11]

Ilia Zdanevich does not seem to have been particularly close to Kruchenykh when both were in the north, but he came to know him well when Kruchenykh lived in the Zdanevich family home in Tiflis from February 1918 to the end of 1919. During this time, in collaboration with the writer Igor Terentev, they founded the Fantastic Tavern, a night-club where they gave lectures and poetry readings. Some of the lectures provided texts for Kruchenykh's books: during two productive years, he produced many titles.[12] Although he used techniques such as typewriting and handwriting reproduced by hectography, as he had before, few of the Tiflis publications are as inventive as his earlier Futurist books, with some exceptions. One is the anthology dedicated by habitués of the Fantastic Tavern to Sofia Georgievna Melnikova.[13] The cover by Kirill Zdanevich [18] is decorated with his drawing of an elaborate bridal crown for this actress, who was the centre of local avant-garde society, from the Tiflis Theatre of Miniatures. The book includes poems by the Georgian poet, Grigory Robakidze, who, on a later occasion, wrote a description of the Fantastic Tavern:

МЕЛЬНИКОВОЙ

хазяин

тАниц тхУп

жыних а
жыних б
танцуют
аркестрам

Н. ГОНЧАРОВА
(карандаш)

МНЕ́ПІĬ: МНУ́ПП: МНЕ́ПĬ: МНУ́ПП

МНЕ́ПП: МНУ́ПП: МНЕ́ПĬ: МНУ́ПП

жыних а
уводит асла

19
To Sofia Melnikova, 1919,
p.47: typography by Ilia
Zdanevich with
reproduction of a drawing
by N.Goncharova
(C.104.dd.6).

20
V. Kamensky, *Into the
Bows, Riff-Raff!* [cry of
Volga brigands when
seizing a boat.], 1932,
cover by Fisher
(C.191.a.16).

Tiflis has become a fantastic city. A fantastic city needed a fantastic corner and, on one fine day, at No.12 Rustaveli, in the courtyard, poets and artists opened a Fantastic Tavern which consisted of a small room, meant for ten to fifteen, but which, by some miracle, had about fifty people in it, more women than men. Phantasmagorias [sic] decorated the walls of the room. Virtually every evening the tavern was open and poets and artists read their poems and lectures.[14]

Other contributors to the anthology were the Armenian Futurist, Kara-Darvish (pseudonym of Akop Minaevich Geniian) and the Georgians, Titsian Tabidze and Pavel Iashvili, as well as Ilia Zdanevich, Terentev and Kruchenykh himself. Surprisingly, a poem by Ilia Zdanevich is illustrated with reproductions of small pencil drawings of donkeys by Nataliia Goncharova [19], left over, perhaps, from the pre-Revolutionary era of the Donkey's Tail group, when he had written a book about her.[15] The pages which include these drawings are more remarkable for the typesetting, which is the result of Ilia Zdanevich having enrolled as an apprentice typesetter in Tiflis in autumn 1917. Even though he found he worked too slowly and abandoned his apprenticeship after a year, the experience gave him the expertise to become a pioneer of inventive typography: he influenced the design of all the books with the imprint 41° until he left Tiflis for Paris in 1920. Designs such as the covers of Kruchenykh's *Lacquered Tights (Lakirovannoe triko)*[16] and Terentev's *Fact (Fakt)*[17] represent the originality of Ilia Zdanevich's typography [see 39, 37]. With invasion by the Bolsheviks threatening the independence of Georgia, the members of 41° dispersed in 1920: Kruchenykh took the imprint first to Baku and then on to Moscow, where he described Ilia Zdanevich as the Paris correspondent of 41° and Terentev as its correspondent in Georgia.[18]

Before the opening of the Fantastic Tavern, Kamensky had already returned to Moscow, where, in autumn 1917, he organized the Poets' Cafe in an old laundry on the corner of Tverskoi Boulevard and Nastasinsky Pereulok. He furnished and decorated it with the help of his friends Mayakovsky and Burliuk and the three of them recited poetry there to audiences which included black-marketeers, anarchists and the secret police. Like the Fantastic Tavern in Tiflis, the Poets' Cafe continued the pre-Revolutionary tradition of artistic night-clubs such as the Stray Dog in Petrograd. The Poets' Cafe was financed by money given to Kamensky by his mistress, the wife of a Moscow millionaire baker, whose money enabled him to support Mayakovsky and David Burliuk and Khlebnikov and to set up the publishing firm, *Kitovras*.[19] Kamensky dedicated *His-My Biography of the Great Futurist (Ego-moia biografiia velikogo futurista)*[20] to this Mrs Filippov but its appearance did not continue the promise of his earlier 'ferroconcrete' poems, such as those in the 1914 *Tango with Cows (Tango s korovami)*;[21] he did not again produce books with distinctive covers [20] until the beginning of the 1930s.[22]

It is perhaps surprising that a semblance of 'normal' life continued for as long as six months after the Revolution, but the Poets' Cafe was closed on 14 April 1918. Before then Mayakovsky, Burliuk and Kamensky established a new publishing venture in Moscow, the Association of Socialist Art (*ASIS*), under which Mayakovsky's *Man. Thing (Chelovek. Veshch')* and *Cloud in Trousers (Oblako v shtanakh. Tetraptikh)*[23] came out. They published a *Futurist Gazette (Gazeta futuristov)* under the same imprint,[24] which, with its poems and manifesto, was a reminder of their pre-Revolutionary activities. The gazette looked more like a news sheet than a book, and copies were pasted poster-like on walls and fences, but sales were negligible (even though the publication coincided with an exhibition of paintings on Kuznetsky Most – organized and hung by David Burliuk) so unsold copies were given to friends or handed out by Mayakovsky at his poetry readings. Soon afterwards David Burliuk broke up the editorial board of the paper by leaving Moscow. This was not, however, the end of his role in Russia because he lived for a while in Vladivostok, where he joined a group of Futurists with the name 'Creation'. Aseev and Sergei Tretiakov were among the group, as well as Pavel Neznamov and Nikolai Chuzhak, the latter a stalwart Communist and editor of the local Party newspaper. Over the following years they printed numerous extracts from Mayakovsky's poems in their journal, *Creation (Tvorchestvo)*, which ran to seven issues. Mayakovsky was praised as the outstanding poet of the Russian Revolution in political articles in *Creation* and this provided him with valuable support when the writers returned to Moscow in 1922.[25]

The *Futurist Gazette* had influenced events (if only for a short time) more than pre-Revolutionary Futurist publications. In their 'Manifesto of the Flying Federation of Futurists'[26] Mayakovsky, Kamensky and Burliuk called for the independence of art from the state – in particular, that the Art Academy should be abolished; this took place a month later (on 12 April 1918). They suggested that artists should decorate 'the ever onrushing flocks of railroad cars' and a first propaganda train set out from Moscow some months later. They demanded a new method of teaching by means of Free Art Studios; the first one opened in Petrograd the following October. In addition to practical proposals, the manifesto called for a Revolution of the Spirit to match political revolution; this eluded Mayakovsky and his friends, as did a similar idea independently put forward by the Symbolist poet Aleksandr Blok and by the Proletarian Cultural and Educational Organization (*Proletkult*).[27]

Other members of the avant-garde – including Tatlin and Malevich – had taken up more overtly political activities in 1917 and joined the Soviets of Soldiers' and Workers' Deputies which effectively ruled Moscow between February and October 1917 when the Provisional Government held power. They supported the formation of a Soviet of Artists' Unions of Moscow, which soon split into three sections, with the avant-garde relegated to the 'junior' one. This Soviet decided to publish a journal of political commentary and the arts, *The Path of Liberation (Put' osvobozhdeniia)*; it was planned as a bi-weekly but only four numbers were published, the last in mid-October.[28] Surprisingly, a newspaper with the title *Anarchy (Anarkhiia)* was initiated in February 1918 and ran to forty-five issues before being closed down in April.[29] Malevich contributed to several issues and one of his articles was subsequently reprinted in *Art of the Commune (Iskusstvo kommuny)*.[30] This was one of two newspapers put out by Futurists, who were now working within *IZO* (the Visual Arts department of the Commissariat of the Enlightenment): *Art of the Commune* was based in Petrograd [21], *Art (Iskusstvo)* in Moscow.[31] In these newspapers, poems declaimed by Mayakovsky were printed instead of editorials and lines of his poetry served as headlines. The poet made a point of appearing before proletarian audiences whenever he could; he first read 'Left March' at the Sailors' Theatre in Petrograd on 17 December 1918 and it was printed on 12 January 1919 in *Art of the Commune*, No.7.[32] Lunacharsky found it hard to countenance the activities of the Futurists and his distrust was published in *Art of the Commune* No.4:

21
Art of the Commune, No.4,
1918, newspaper mast-
head, designer
unidentified (C.191.c.6).

22
Fine Art No.1, [1920] cover
by D. Shterenberg
(LR.416.tt.10).

Two features of the young face of your paper, in whose pages my letter is printed, frighten me: its destructive tendencies in relation to the past, and its attempt, in speaking in the name of a definite school, to speak at the same time in the name of the government ... It would be wrong if the artist-innovators presumed to regard themselves as a government artistic school, working for an official, even though revolutionary, art dictated from above.[33]

None the less he had given his approval for the founding of the imprint *IMO (Iskusstvo molodykh)* in July 1918[34] and Mayakovsky published his collected poems[35] and an anthology, *The 'New' Word (Rzhanoe slovo)*, with a foreword by Lunacharsky under this imprint.[36] An agreement with the Commissariat meant that no fee was paid until the books were sold; this forced Mayakovsky to rely on his public appearances as an opportunity to sell his books, until the form of agreement was changed in February 1919, and fees were paid on submission of a manuscript.[37] In a bid for greater political acceptance, Mayakovsky attempted, with Brik, to set up a Communist Futurist Collective (*Kom-fut*) in the Vyborg District of Petrograd. The third issue of *Art of the Commune* carries a note about a preparatory meeting and a *Kom-fut* manifesto appeared in issue No.10, of 1918.[38] Their attempt proved fruitless because at the end of January 1919 the Vyborg District Party Committee decided not to register *Kom-fut* as a Party Collective, so the Futurists failed to establish an official platform. Furthermore, they were excluded from the May Day celebrations of 1919.

In spite of rebuffs, an illustrated journal with contributions by principal members of the avant-garde was planned in 1918 to run in parallel with the newspapers *Art of the Commune* and *Art*. After considerable delay, the journal (though dated 1919) came out in a single number early in 1920. It was called simply, *Fine Art (Izobrazitel'noe iskusstvo* No.1),[39] connecting it in the minds of readers with *IZO*, and, without doubt, this helped to foster the notion that avant-garde art was the instrument of the Party. The cover has a sober Cubist design by Shterenberg [22] and *Fine Art* included good-quality photographs of

paintings and sculpture by the principal avant-garde artists, including Malevich and Tatlin. It served as a herald of new Russian art in Western Europe, where it bears comparison with the spate of avant-garde journals published in the early 1920s. In 1918 and 1919 a few avant-garde artists also succeeded in having well-printed monographs devoted to their work (these will be discussed in Chapter 5), but illustrated books devoted exclusively to visual art were rare. Nevertheless, avant-garde artists gained positions of responsibility which had eluded them in previous years. As a sculptor, Tatlin was a beneficiary on all counts: in 1919 he was commissioned to design a Monument to the Third International which was described in detail by Punin in the booklet of the same title (*Pamiatnik III Internationala*).[40] Tatlin's project for a huge tower, reproduced on the cover [see 76], became the most widely recognized icon of the period, since the design was reproduced in the next few years in several avant-garde European journals.[41] Like Malevich, Tatlin held various administrative posts including that of Master in the Free Art Studios set up in 1918. It is, however, a common mistake to over-rate the popularity of the avant-garde at this time: when invited to cast votes for Studio Masters in 1918 students gave eighty-eight votes to the realist, Abram Arkhipov, and thirty-five for the moderate, Pavel Kuznetsov; in contrast, Tatlin gained eight and Malevich only four.[42]

The discussion so far has centred on Futurists, but mention must be made of their rivals in Proletkult, with whom they had some connections. Proletkult was set up early in 1917 with Bogdanov (pseudonym of Aleksandr Malinovsky) as its head. Proletarian art for Bogdanov was not simply 'the representation of life from a proletarian point of view', but 'a means of organizing the forces of the proletariat as a class for its historic mission of building socialism through collective labour.'[43] He saw the role of Proletkult as being separate from government and Party; indeed, by remaining separate, it could later reconstruct government. The Party, however, saw the independence of the organization as a threat and, in 1920, following a tactless speech by Lunacharsky to a Proletkult Congress advocating their full autonomy, Lenin forced the Party Central Committee to pass a resolution putting the organization under Lunacharsky's control.[44] The resolution was to have far reaching effects, for it stated that a proletarian culture could arise only on the basis of existing 'bourgeois' thought and culture, thereby affirming tradition and indirectly attacking Futurists who wanted art to begin afresh from new foundations. Proletkult continued its educational role as a subordinate body within *Narkompros*, holding classes in the arts and literature for workers and organizing theatrical productions (discussed in Chapter 4). It was a powerful body, for in 1920 there were about eighty thousand people studying in Proletkult studios throughout the country, with old guard writers such as the Symbolists, Bely and Valery Briusov, teaching courses for poets and writers.[45]

Poets with a proletarian background formed circles within Proletkult and, in Moscow, a breakaway group, 'The Smithy' (*Kuznitsa*), was led by Aleksei Gastev. His poetry extols factory life – iron girders and men who merge with the iron[46] – and he attempted to apply to writing some of the methods applied to industry by the American efficiency expert, Frederick Winslow Taylor. In the United States Taylor had demonstrated that industrial output could be increased by scientific management: he had analyzed production methods and trained workers to make their bodily movements as appropriate as possible to the task in

СУМЭ-ЧЕНГ

КИТАЯНКА СУМЭ- -ЧЕНГ

ГОСИЗДАТ

Plate 4
N.N.Aseev,
V.V.Mayakovsky, *The
Story of How Akim coped
with Misfortune*, 1925
(C.114.mm.52).

hand; he had also introduced piece work.[47] Although subsequent research has shown that Taylor often achieved his successes by finding well-motivated, strong individuals whose efforts could not be matched by the average worker,[48] the principles of Taylorism fitted the needs of the new Soviet government, for it was proving more difficult to manage industry than the Communists had hoped. In the 1920s Gastev was put in charge of a Central Institute of Labour (*TsIT*) where he practised and developed Taylor's ideas. Lunacharsky commended Gastev as 'heralding the beginning of an epoch of pure technology and, following Taylor's footsteps … introducing the idea of subordinating people to mechanisms, of the mechanization of man.'[49]

Gastev's poetry and theoretical articles seem today to dehumanize workers as much as to praise them. He hailed mechanization not only of the worker's body – by gestures in production – but also of the mind – by mechanization of everyday thinking. This, he said, 'gives proletarian psychology a striking anonymity which allows one to qualify the individual proletarian unit as A,B,C or as 325.075 and 0, etc.' His article, published in *Proletarian Culture (Proletarskaia kul'tura)*[50] includes a 'Taylorized' chart of four kinds of workers in the metal-working industry. Lunacharsky's rather similar support for the collective over the individual is expressed more fully in a pamphlet published in English in 1919, where he outlined the 'Cultural task of the Struggling Proletariat':

> *We must bear in mind that the struggle is one for an ideal: that of the culture of brotherhood and complete freedom; of victory over the individualism which cripples human beings; and of a communal life based not on compulsion and the need of man to herd together for mere self-preservation, as it was in the past, but on a free and natural merging of personalities into super-personal entities.*[51]

Although the Futurists are usually seen as rivals to Proletkult and the Smithy, books and journals provide evidence of connections and shared interests and for a short time in 1920 they gained influence in Proletkult.[52] Links persisted and in 1923 the Constructivist artist, Gustav Klutsis, redesigned the cover of the Proletkult journal, *The Furnace (Gorn)*,[53] replacing an old-fashioned design with bold, sans-serif lettering which he ran across the width of the cover [23a, b]. Mayakovsky was an occasional contributor to *The Furnace* and, later on, while a member of *LEF*, Tretiakov also wrote plays for and directed the Proletkult theatre. Futurist writers and artists were not immune to the Smithy poets' enthusiasm for the plural hero, 'we', replacing the singular 'I' of the past, and they shared an interest in Taylorism. Rodchenko made seventeen costume designs for a play by Aleksei Gan entitled *We (My)* in 1920,[54] and, in 1925, designed a cover for a book by Taylor.[55] Although it would be imprudent to posit more direct links between Rodchenko and Taylorism itself, he produced distinctive covers for a series of technical books published under the imprint *Transpechat'*.[56] Rodchenko's interest in technical subjects was sincere, for one of his students remembered his talking to them about scientific subjects and his taking them to a lecture at the Polytechnical Museum about radio broadcasting[57] – the subject of another book for which he designed the cover.[58] In the theatre, Meyerhold was directly inspired by Taylor, basing his system for training actors – which he called 'biomechanics' – on the American's ideas; this is discussed further in Chapter 4.

The United States was not the only foreign country to provide a formative influence on emergent culture in Soviet Russia.[59] In the field of

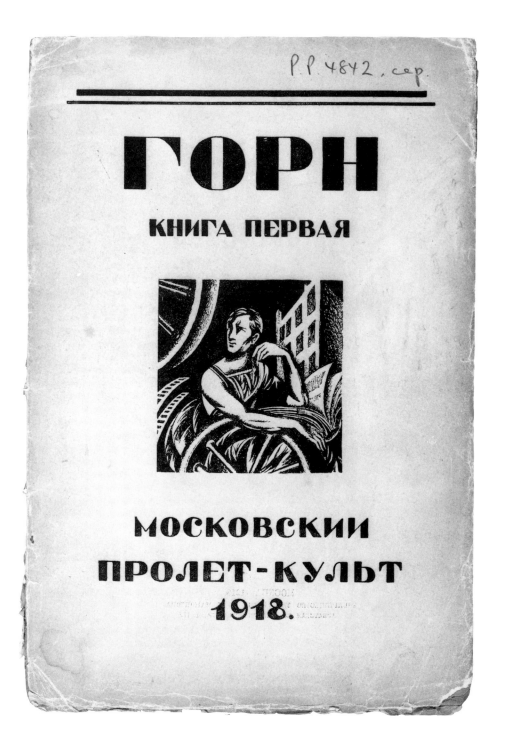

typography there seems to have been early links with Germany and Hungary. In book covers, an early example of a 'purer' style of typography is to be found in the design of two volumes of Mayakovsky's collected works, *13 Years of Work (13 let raboty)*,[60] carried out by Lavinsky, the Head of Sculpture at *VKhUTEMAS*, late in 1922 [24]. He employed large sans-serif capitals, in two colours, and underlined the name 'Mayakovsky'; both these devices are much closer to the green and orange lettering on a cover by George Grosz for his book, *With Scissors and Brush (Mit Pinsel und Schere, 7 Materialisationen)*,[61] than to any previous Russian design, though Lavinsky ranged his words to the left instead of centering them as on the German cover. It seems likely that Grosz's book – of photographic reproductions of his watercolours and collages – was known in Moscow, as the artist was sent to Russia for five months in the summer of 1922 by the German branch of the International Workers' Aid organization.[62] A second parallel is to be found in the typographic cover of a new Hungarian art journal, *Unity (Egység)*, which was founded in Vienna in May 1922 under the editorship of the Communist writer Aladár Komját and artist, Béla Uitz.[63] Uitz had spent at least seven months in Moscow from January to June 1921 at a time of intense debate at the Institute of Artistic Culture (*INKhUK*) (discussed further in Chapter 5); he was close to Rodchenko and is likely to have sent copies of the magazine to Moscow. Due to the language barrier the typography and reproductions would have had more impact in Moscow than articles in the magazine.

The year 1922 saw increasing exchange of information about avant-garde art between the Soviet Union and Western Europe. Publications printed in Berlin brought up-to-date news to artists in a language they could understand. Thus the writer Ilia Erenburg's book, *And Yet the World Goes Round (A vse taki ona vertitsia)*[64] – with a striking cover by Fernand Léger composed from stencilled letters and machine-like forms – included information about the principal European avant-garde art journals, including their own, by then out of date, *Fine Art* [see 22]. Lissitzky played a decisive role: he had studied in Germany before the Revolution and was fluent in the language and 'European' in outlook. He moved from Moscow to Berlin in December 1921 and the following spring joined Erenburg to found and edit an ambitious international journal, *Object (Veshch'. Gegendstand. Objet)*.[65] Only two issues were published (Nos.1/2, March/April and No.3, May) although a fourth – to be devoted to Russian art – was announced, as well as a fifth, to American art. During 1922 Lissitzky and Erenburg disseminated information about the latest developments in Russian avant-garde art in the principal European art journals, for which Lissitzky often contributed the design.[66] At the same time he corresponded with Russian artists, so Moscow was closely linked to the rest of Europe. Mayakovsky also served as a go-between, bringing back publications and art materials on his numerous visits abroad; his first visit to Berlin and Paris took place in October-November 1922 when work by Soviet artists of all trends was on view in Berlin at the 'First Russian Exhibition' at the van Diemen Gallery.[67] There was disappointment that more avant-garde work was not shown, but Russians could see that their abstract art rivalled any being produced in Western Europe, despite years of isolation brought about by the Great War, Revolution and Civil War, and Lissitzky's powerful catalogue cover proclaimed their strength in book design.[68]

During 1922 Mayakovsky was closely connected with *VKhUTEMAS* which produced books by himself and Kruchenykh under the imprint 'Moscow

МАЯКОВСКИЙ

13
ЛЕТ
РАБО=
ТЫ

ТОМ 1

Association of Futurists' (*MAF*). (By this time Kruchenykh had returned to Moscow from the south.) The uniform design of six *MAF* books of poetry and theory gives them a certain authority [25], perhaps reflecting the support that the Moscow Futurists received in 1922 when the Creation group – mentioned earlier, p.45 – returned from the Far East and settled in Moscow. In December Mayakovsky and Osip Brik began discussions with the new arrivals about forming a group, to be named the 'Left Front of Arts' (*LEF*).[69] *LEF* proved a stronger and more enduring group than *Kom-fut* or *MAF* and, as well as publishing books, initiated a journal, *LEF*, which ran to seven issues between April 1923 and the beginning of 1925.[70]

During its first years of publication *LEF* served as a unifying force among members. The first number included the text of Brik's *Not a Fellow Traveller (Ne poputchitsa)*[71] and Mayakovsky's *About This (Pro eto)*[72] – both of them published by *LEF* under separate covers later in the year. The cover of Brik's *Not a Fellow Traveller* – with its bold lettering arranged on a diagonal to echo a cut-out photograph of a speeding train [26] – was executed by Lavinsky, who based it on an earlier idea by Mayakovsky.[73] No doubt the image was intended to represent Brik's firm commitment to the Revolution compared with the uncertainty of a 'fellow traveller' – a term invented by Trotsky to describe writers who 'are not the artists of the proletarian revolution but its artistic fellow travellers'.[74] The partnership between Mayakovsky and this designer was eclipsed during 1923, however, by the poet's new partnership with Rodchenko, with whom he embarked on a series of posters advertising State industries.[75] This led to a fruitful collaboration on books and journals: one of the first was *LEF*, with Mayakovsky as editor and Rodchenko as designer [*see* 86 and plate 1].

The journal was the most impressive that the Futurists had ever published. The first three issues ran to several hundred pages each[76] and, as well as original fiction, included criticism and policy statements such as, 'Futurism stands to the left front of art' (*LEF* No.1, p.4). The journal was intended for foreign consumption: when plans were being made for the new journal, foreign correspondents, including Grosz, Tristan Tzara and Robert Delaunay, were suggested.[77] *LEF* was evidently intended to be of more than local interest: No.2 includes a manifesto-like editorial: 'Comrades – Organizers of Life!' printed in Russian, German, and English. Foreign works of art were, however, rarely reproduced – in No.2 there were two drawings by Grosz; in No.4 – of August 1924 – there was a photomontage by Paul Citroën, then working at the Bauhaus.

LEF inevitably came under fire for its 'incomprehensibility to the masses' which may account for the reduction in the print-run and the increasing irregularity of publication. During 1924 its look underwent a change: colour reproductions of textile designs by Popova were reproduced in memory of her untimely death from scarlet fever that year, and they coincided with preparations for the Soviet contribution to the international exhibition of decorative arts (*Exposition Internationale des Arts décoratifs et industriels modernes*) held in Paris in 1925. The catalogue[78] for the section on Soviet design was the work of Rodchenko, but in spite of winning a silver medal for book design,[79] he seems to have found his visit to Paris disappointing. None the less he made good use of the Leica camera that he acquired in Western Europe and began to use it to take his own truly remarkable photographs. For the cover of Mayakovsky's poem *Paris (Parizh)*[80] he used an aerial photograph of the city, which may have inspired the inventive viewpoints which became characteristic of his own photographs.

А. КРУЧЕНЫХ.

МАФ

МОСКОВСКАЯ —
В БУДУЩЕМ МЕ-
ЖДУНАРОДНАЯ —
АССОЦИАЦИЯ
ФУТУРИСТОВ.

ФАКТУРА СЛОВА.

СЕРИЯ
ТЕОРИИ

№ 1.

МОСКВА,
1923.

МАРИЕНГОФ

ИВНЕВ

ИМАЖИНИСТЫ

РОЙЗМАН

ШЕРШЕНЕВИЧ

ИЗДАНИЕ АВТОРОВ, МОСКВА, ТЕАТРАЛЬНЫЙ ПРОЕЗД. 2.

◁ **26**
O. Brik, *Not a Fellow Traveller*, 1923, cover by A. Lavinsky (Cup.408.g.24).

27
Imaginists, 1925, cover by G. Stenberg (C.191.b.4).

28

A. Kruchenykh, *Esenin the Hooligan* (11872.pp.15); *Esenin's Dark Secret* (C.136.b.31); *Esenin and Moscow of the Taverns* (C.191.a.15); *Esenin's Death* (C.191.a.14), all 1926.

The quality of Rodchenko's photographs can be seen in the covers which he designed in 1926 for Mayakovsky's book dedicated *To Sergei Esenin (Sergeiu Eseninu)*.[81] As a person and as a poet Esenin was the antithesis of Mayakovsky. Whereas Mayakovsky had abandoned the country setting of his childhood, preferring to live in and write about the modern city, Esenin had remained at heart close to his village roots. In 1920 in his prose work, *Mary's Keys (Kliuchi Marii)*, he wrote 'we have made almost all things around us live and pray' and he regretted the passing of peasants as 'the keepers of (cosmic) mysteries'.[82]

Esenin's first collection of poems was published in 1916 and he joined the Imaginist group, with Shershenevich, Mariengof and Aleksandr Kusikov; they published a manifesto in February 1919.[83] The group initially supported the Revolution and considered themselves to be to the left of the Futurists. Imaginists sought the primacy of 'the image' in poetry, hoping to think in images; they maintained that a poem is not an organism but an agglomeration of images; their pessimism and use of coarse language exceeded that of the Futurists. In 1925 they published their anthology, *Imaginists (Imaginisty)*,[84] with a cover by Georgy Stenberg [27]. Esenin's photograph does not appear on this cover but he was caught up by the Imaginists, though his poetry is greatly superior to that of the rest of the group. He is probably best known in the West for his dramatic marriage to Isadora Duncan and their world tour in 1922; during this period his alcoholism was at its worst and when he returned alone to Russia he could find no comfort in the countryside, changed so profoundly in the aftermath of Revolution. In December 1925 he cut his wrists, wrote a farewell poem in his own blood, and then hanged himself from a radiator pipe in a room of the Hotel Angleterre in Leningrad. The dramatic incident shocked the literary world – particularly young Communists who had admired the 'hooliganism' of his poetry – and the event subsequently inspired a great deal of material for publication; Kruchenykh used the event as the excuse for at least six books [28].[85] Mayakovsky spoke out against the suicide though he succumbed to death by his own hand himself less than five years afterwards. At the time, Esenin's death seemed a victory for those who believed that the Revolution marked the end of individualism and the beginning of a new era of the collective, and 'Eseninism' was described as a 'disease' which could undermine the new society.[86] In his covers for Mayakovsky's *To Sergei Esenin*, Rodchenko emphasized the clash between town and countryside, by cutting circular photographs of wheat and an *izba* (a peasant's wooden house) and superimposing the first on a railway bridge for the front cover and the second on a 'worm's eye view' of a block of flats for the back cover.[87] Rodchenko used photographs to great advantage on the covers of a redesigned *LEF* – *New LEF (Novyi LEF)* – which began publication in 1927; he served as the designer for all the numbers in 1927 and 1928 and each of them is distinguished by his remarkable photographs [29], arranged in a telling way.[88]

Though it looks so different from the earlier periodical, *New LEF* was still the organ of the *LEF* group and still adhered to the ideology of the group. It was, however, soon beset with differences between the editor, Mayakovsky, and his contributors, particularly Tretiakov, who replaced him as editor after the seventh issue (of July 1928). Some of the grounds for dispute can be seen in 'a first anthology by the workers of *LEF*' which came out under the title, *Literature of Fact (Literatura fakta)* in 1929.[89] The book [30] contained articles written in the previous two years by the editor, Chuzhak, as well as by Tretiakov, Brik, Shklovsky and

А. КРУЧЕНЫХ.

ХУЛИ ГАН

ЕСЕН ИН

ИЗД. АВТОРА   МОСКВА 1926

А. КРУЧЕНЫХ

ЧОРНАЯ ТАЙНА
ЕСЕНИНА

ИЗДАНИЕ АВТОРА
МОСКВА   1926

А. КРУЧЕНЫХ.

ЕСЕНИН
и МОСКВА
КАБАЦКАЯ

Третье дополненное издание
ИЗДАНИЕ АВТОРА
Москва—1926

А. Крученых

ГИБЕЛЬ
ЕСЕНИНА

ИЗДАНИЕ АВТОРА
Москва—1926

ФАКТА

ЛИТЕРАТУРА

ПЕРВЫЙ СБОРНИК
МАТЕРИАЛОВ

РАБОТНИКОВ
ЛЕФА

ФЕДЕРАЦИЯ

◁ **29**
New LEF, No.6, 1927, cover
by A. Rodchenko
(C.104.dd.51).

30
Literature of Fact, 1929,
cover, designer
unidentified (11858.bbb.4).

31
P. Neznamov, *All's Well on the Street*, 1929, cover by A. Rodchenko. (Cup. 408.d.34).

32
S. Tretiakov, *Altogether, Verses*, 1924, cover by A. Rodchenko (11588.h.27).

Neznamov amongst others, who extolled 'factual literature' as an antidote to fiction, seeing newspapers as the present-day alternative to epics.[90]

Mayakovsky was against the notion of literature as fact which he saw as a side-track, and by May 1929 he had planned an alternative to *LEF* – the Revolutionary Front of Art (*REF*) – with his closest friends and associates. These included Aseev, Brik, Neznamov and Semen Kirsanov, as well as Rodchenko and Stepanova. *REF* held an inaugural evening in October, its first and last public gathering.[91] The 'reform' was not, however, in the direction required by the Party in the light of the First Five Year Plan, discussed in the Introduction. It became clear that the 'true' party line belonged to the Russian Association of Proletarian Writers (*RAPP*) when the Resolution of the Central Committee 'On the serving of the mass reader with literature' was issued in December 1928.[92] At the time of the opening of his exhibition, 'Twenty Years of Work' (discussed at the beginning of this chapter),[93] Mayakovsky quarrelled with *REF* and, at the *RAPP* conference later in February, he applied to join the organization, maintaining that he had never 'had any disagreements as to the literary-political line of the Party'.[94] His membership was accepted reluctantly – he was clearly too much of an individual to be capable of conforming to the narrow 'orthodoxy' of *RAPP*, which was dominated by younger, Communist writers. He must himself have realized the falseness of his move. In April, after writing a suicide note taking full responsibility for his action, he shot himself in the head.[95]

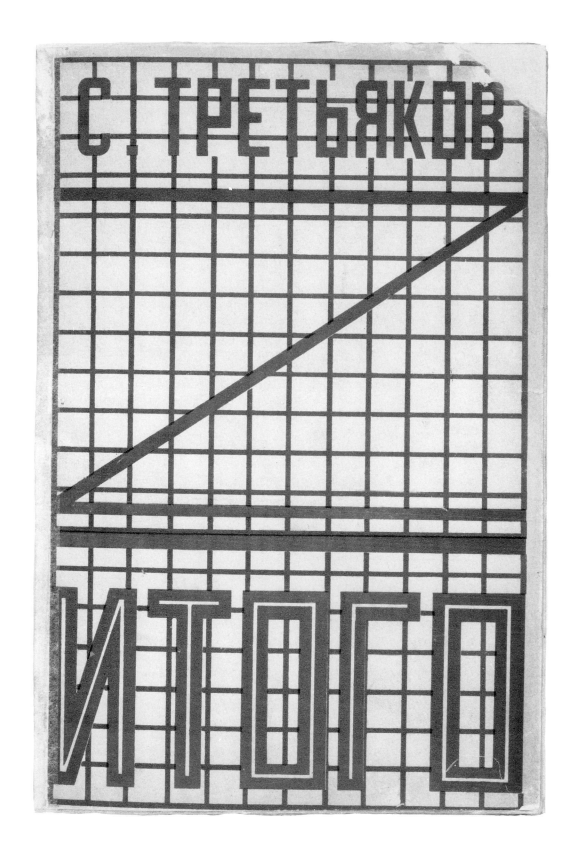

С. ТРЕТЬЯКОВ

ИТОГО

Mayakovsky's death removed the most vociferous member of the avant-garde, an untameable prophet whose books had shaped the sound and look of literature. His partnership with Rodchenko had resulted in the distinctive covers which advertized his work in the 1920s, but the younger man had proved less concerned with the literary disagreements which contributed to Mayakovsky's suicide, for he continued to work with Tretiakov on *New LEF* (after Mayakovsky had resigned) until the demise of the journal. Rodchenko did, however, join Mayakovsky's *REF*, but the cover [31] which he designed for a volume of Neznamov's poems, *All's Well on the Street (Khorosho na ulitse)*,[96] marked no new development in style. Instead, it is firmly based on designs he had made at the inception of Constructivism in art, namely the grid pattern he had drawn by hand on a copy of the catalogue for the first exhibition of Constructivist graphics in 1921.[97] A grid had also formed the basis of his cover for Tretiakov's *Altogether. Verses (Itogo. Stikhi)*[98] in 1924 [32], so it represents a thread running through his Constructivist book design in the 1920s.

When Constructivism in literature joined Constructivism in the visual arts Rodchenko used a typographic design for the cover of the group's first anthology, which they named *All Change (Mena vsekh)*.[99] The young writers, led by Ilia Selvinsky and Kornely Zelinsky, had formed a Literary Centre of Constructivists (*LTsK*) and their declaration was printed in *LEF* in 1925.[100] *LTsK* did not share the extremism of theorists such as Brik and Boris Arvatov, who advocated the extension of Constructivism into Productivism in books such as *Production Art (Iskusstvo v proizvodstve)*[101] and *Art and Class (Iskusstvo i klassy)*,[102] but they believed that writers should project 'into their work upon verbal material the formal and technical achievements of the epoch' as they wrote in *All Change*.[103] In some respects these writers were close to artists, for instance, when, in the same book, they upheld that 'Constructivism is a school which stands on a firm foundation of science and mathematics'.[104] Their dictum is borne out by Rodchenko's forceful cover design [33], developed from the design he had made for the title-page of *LEF* which he strengthened by printing the title letters on a dark ground.

The status of Constructivism – seen as a position upheld by artists and writers at the time – can be deduced from the fact that this design for *All Change* and a second one by Rodchenko were reproduced among examples of the latest approach to book covers in a 1926 volume on Soviet printing and publications.[105] However, the second cover by Rodchenko – reproduced bottom right on the same plate [*see* 33] – for the Russian translation of a book about revolution by the French Socialist, Henri Barbusse[106] – shows a photograph of soldiers overprinted by the title. It is a straightforward approach to cover design, which seems surprisingly close to the Socialist Realism which ousted Constructivism and all other modernist movements early in the next decade.

As has been discussed in the Introduction, a variety of approach was sustained for most of the 1920s and a second anthology by Constructivist poets, *State Plan for Literature (GOSPLAN literatury)*,[107] came out in 1925. Its cover was designed by Nikolai Kupreianov, who closely followed Rodchenko's example; the title was exceptionally pertinent at this time of discussion on the status of literature in a Communist society.[108] The book contains an insert, with a newspaper-like format, entitled *LTsK News (Izvestiia LTsK)* with a montage of photographs of the faces of the principal contributors superimposed on cartoon-

НОВОЕ ЛИЦО
С С С Р

1

like bodies.[109] The joke suggests that the choice of title for the anthology should not be taken as a serious proposition that the Constructivists' plan was in some sense a State-approved plan for literature.

The Literary Centre of Constructivists retained connections with Constructivist artists. The technical virtuosity of Lissitzky's photographic cover [see 53] for Selvinsky's *Notes of a Poet (Zapiski poeta)*[110] contrasts with the simple cover design for another book by the same writer, a narrative poem about the defeat of an anarchist, Sergei Ulialaev, by a Communist during the Civil War, *The Ulialaev Adventure (Ulialaevshchina),*[111] printed in 1927. Its cover was made from a tartan design, printed in shades of brown, resembling designs for Constructivist checked fabrics made by Stepanova in 1924;[112] the connection remains uncertain as the cover is signed with unidentified roman letters, 'JR' [34]. The cover of a 1929 anthology by the same group, entitled *Business (Biznes),* with a photomontage of a large pair of spectacles superimposed on a view of skyscrapers, has been ascribed to Rodchenko.[113] The imagery illustrates Zelinsky's view that American technological skills must be acquired for the successful modernization of the Soviet Union: 'The West again rises before us – not now as a "well of ideas" ... but more as a box of instruments without which ... one cannot build a barn, let alone socialism.'[114] At the time of publication Constructivist architects were able better to appreciate American technology than writers, who may, however, have derived some of their ideas from the pages of the journal, *Contemporary Architecture (Sovremennaia arkhitektura)*[115] to be discussed in Chapter 5.

By the time the First Five Year Plan was under way, there was a general hardening of attitude against radical art of any kind. Among the younger avant-garde, an element of realism returned to book design – an outstanding example being Solomon Telingater's design of Aleksandr Bezymensky's poem *Komsomol (Komsomoliia),* published in 1928 by the Union of Communist Youth.[116] Telingater's inventive combination of typography and photography placed in parallel columns stems in part from his partnership with Lissitzky on the design of a catalogue [see 10] for the All-Union Printing exhibition held in Moscow the year before.[117] Since Lissitzky had had the widest experience of printing of any book designer in Russia, Telingater had an excellent training. None the less, his light-hearted design for *Kirsanov is Called upon to Speak (Slovo predostavliaetsia Kirsanovu)*[118] of 1931 seems like a surprising throwback to Dadaism [plate 5]. An altogether more assured approach is seen on the title-page which he had made for *Contemporary Architecture* the year before [see 81], though this was formed directly from a dramatic proposal for a Palace of Culture for the Proletarsky district of Moscow by the Constructivist architect Ivan Leonidov.[119] Extreme designs like this one brought upon Constructivist architecture the tag 'Leonidovism' (*leonidovshchina*) from more conservative members of the profession.

In reaction to criticism Leonidov pushed design to Utopian limits but other members of the avant-garde reacted in different ways. At the end of the 1920s Kruchenykh devoted his time to reproducing unpublished material by Khlebnikov in 'samizdat' format, using similar methods to ones he had used before the Revolution [see 17]. Although the books were not suppressed, they were hand-made in very small editions for the 'friends of Khlebnikov'.[120] At the time it seemed equally appropriate to revive Mayakovsky's *ROSTA* posters after his suicide. Stepanova designed an up-to-date collection of couplets and illustrations,

Обложка к книге Г. Зиновьева о В. И. Ленине.
1924.

Обложка А. Родченко.

Обложка А. Родченко.

Обложка Дени к сборнику его карикатур.
1923. Госиздат.

Н·О·В·О·С·Т·И
РУССКОЙ
ЛИТЕРАТУРЫ

ИЛЬЯ СЕЛЬВИНСКИЙ

УЛЯЛАЕВЩИНА

ЭПОПЕЯ

АРТЕЛЬ ПИСАТЕЛЕЙ „КРУГ" 1927

◁ **33**
M. Shchelkunov, *History, Technique and Art of Book Printing*, 1926, p.423: top right: H. Barbusse, *Speeches of a Fighter*, 1924, bottom left, *All Change*, 1924, both covers by A. Rodchenko (2705.a.11).

34
I. Selvinsky, *The Ulialaev Adventure*, 1927, cover initialled 'J.R.' (11595.c.53).

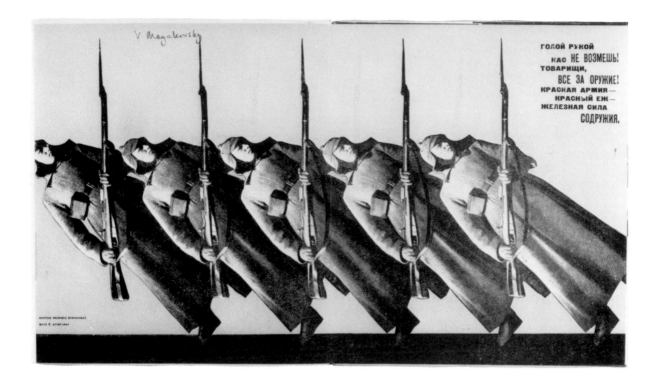

ГОЛОЙ РУКОЙ
НАС НЕ ВОЗМЕШЬ!
ТОВАРИЩИ,
ВСЕ ЗА ОРУЖИЕ!
КРАСНАЯ АРМИЯ —
КРАСНЫЙ ЕЖ —
ЖЕЛЕЗНАЯ СИЛА
СОДРУЖИЯ.

35
V. Mayakovsky, *Menacing
Laughter*, 1932, endpapers
by V. Stepanova
(C.127.d.21).

36
F. Panferov, *Bruski* (A Story
of Peasant Life in Soviet
Russia), vol.2, 1931, cover,
designer unidentified
(12590.t.1).

with the title, *Menacing Laughter (Groznyi smekh)*,[121] packaging the whole in
striking covers and endpapers [35] which she designed herself. Notwithstanding
the uncertainties of the times, Lissitzky gave a surprisingly optimistic lecture on
book design at the Moscow House of the Press. According to the report in the
journal, *Artists' Brigade (Brigada khudozhnikov)*, he reminded his audience that
even before it is read, a book should create an impression of quality. Looking back
to the years before 1917 he remembered the lavish look of World of Art
publications and compared it to the sober look of post-revolutionary,
Constructivist publications. He went on to propose a programme for
contemporary books, maintaining that 'the form of the book is by no means
determined solely by the sensibilities of taste'. However, he approved of a certain
amount of standardization to prevent each book in an exhibition trying to 'shout
down its neighbour' – perhaps unwittingly setting a pattern for the less
distinguished design of Soviet books, including his own, in the later 1930s:
Socialist Industry (Industriia sotsializma), of 1935, is a pretentious set of seven,
separately bound parts [plate 6] with poor quality photographs.[122]

In the early 1930s the increasingly strict laws on censorship
additionally applied to the appearance of books (described in the Introduction)
naturally resulted in a decline in inventiveness in design. The deterioration is
vividly demonstrated by a popular novel by Fedor Panferov, *Bruski* (A Story of
Peasant Life in Soviet Russia), which came out in four volumes between 1931 and
1937.[123] The author's aim was to persuade his reader of the advantage of collective
farming over individual land holding. The first two volumes were brought out in
1931 by *RAPP* and were immensely popular; the novel was acclaimed as a classic
of Soviet literature. Before the third volume was ready the publishers – the

ф. панферов

бруски

кн. 2

гихл · 1931

Новинки Пролетарской Литературы

Association of Proletarian Writers – had been disbanded with all other literary and artistic groupings,[124] so the third and fourth volumes were accredited to *Gosizdat*. The appearance of each volume exactly matches the hardening of censorship: the first, described as a 'Five Year Plan' novel in a series entitled 'Soviet Proletarian Literature', has a cover decorated with a straightforward photograph of a rural scene with tractors; volume two has a slightly more adventurous design – a photomontage dominated by the benign faces of a group of peasant women [36]. The two further volumes reflect the hardening against innovation: they are encased in plain brown rexine hard covers of a kind which became characteristic of Soviet books. Volume three is the only illustrated one, with reproductions of drawings by the Socialist Realist artist Boris Ioganson, but this was not the creative partnership between a writer and an artist whose work complements each other. Ioganson's style has a strong moral flavour – which looks like a throwback to art produced by the Wanderers group (*Peredvizhniki*) in the nineteenth and early twentieth centuries.[125] In the mid-1930s Gorky criticized Panferov's poor craftsmanship and his opinion was backed by many critics but Panferov proudly retorted that he could learn more from technical works on the peat industry than from Tolstoy or Dostoyevsky.[126] One volume was translated into English, with the title *And Then the Harvest*[127] and today it reads as a remarkable portrayal of the decade. It radiates energy with a strange mixture of achievements and disasters following each other in quick succession, as though to hold the readers' attention at all costs. Strangely, little attempt is made to hide the dreadful living conditions and lack of education of most of the workers; only the managers and their wives live in comparative luxury, with cars and live-in helpers. The book has lost all the idealism of the early revolutionary years, its covers no longer need to advertise a new world because for the time being it had come to resemble the old. The fervour of the avant-garde had been tamed; its torch-bearer, Mayakovsky, had silenced himself; paradoxically, only Stalin's decision to perpetuate his memory saved his remarkable achievement from oblivion, and preserved the inventions of his partners in design.

3

Medium and Message:
design, technique and content

There are references to remarkable designs throughout this book, but this chapter is given over to a more detailed investigation of some of the best-known publications, which are also amongst the most original. Rather than discussing them in isolation, they will be connected with closely related books which help to clarify their special quality. The major designers are Rodchenko and Lissitzky, who made commercially produced covers for large editions of books which take their place in history alongside the smaller, de-luxe editions that comprise another aspect of outstanding nineteenth and twentieth century book design. Both had previous experience of handmade books: the books that Lissitzky hand-printed in the Graphics Department at the Vitebsk Art School before he left Soviet Russia in 1921 are mentioned in Chapter 5; discussion of Rodchenko's handmade books belongs here. Rodchenko hand-made his covers for Kruchenykh, whose collaboration with artists had already been responsible for outstanding books in 1912-16.

Between those years and his brief partnership with Rodchenko in 1922, Kruchenykh continued to be involved in book production in Georgia when little publishing was done in Soviet Russia. In his underused capacity as a graphic designer, he made collages. (More often he preferred writing books and relying on artists to provide covers and illustrations for them.) He used collage to decorate the printed cover [plate 7] of some copies of *Obesity of Roses (Ozhirenie roz)*[1] which resembled those in *Universal War (Vselenskaia voina)*, a book that was published in Petrograd in 1916.[2] The similarity has reopened the question of authorship of some collages made before the partnership between Kruchenykh and Rozanova broke up.[3] The collages for *Universal War* were attributed to Rozanova in the previous volume of this study,[4] but books produced afterwards by Kruchenykh suggest that he made the earlier collages himself. Some copies of *1918* – published in Tiflis in 1917 – include a handwritten list of previously published work, with the information, 'A. Kruchenykh, Universal War, coloured collages, out of print' with no mention of Rozanova's name, though the joint authorship of other books is credited in the same list.[5]

By far the most important new departure was the development of commercial printing by Ilia Zdanevich, who played a part in the design of all books issued in Tiflis under the imprint 41° – the association of Kruchenykh, Kirill and Ilia Zdanevich and Terentev described in Chapter 2. Among the most striking publications is Terentev's *Fact (Fakt)*[6] with its dramatic cover design [37] of varying sized letters arranged in an irregular way and emphasized by printers' hands, traditionally seen on circus posters. Such devices had appeared in 1913 on a poster advertising the first evening of Russian Futurists[7] but Ilia Zdanevich's free use of similar ones is more likely due to his experience as an apprentice in a printers' shop, where he handled Ukrainian as well as Russian founts and explored the range of ready-made printers' signs. In the end he found the process so time-consuming that he reverted to working in the usual way by giving instructions to the printers for the layout of type and decorations. His professionalism can be judged by comparing the covers for *Kruchenykh the Grandiozaire (Kruchenykh grandiozar')*[8] – bearing a rather nondescript drawing by Kirill Zdanevich [38] – with Ilia's typographic design [39] of *Lacquered Tights (Lakirovannoe triko)*.[9]

An antecedent to the second design may be found in the cover of a book by Carlo Carrà, *Guerrapittura*, published in Milan in 1915 with equally bold typography arranged in dynamic diagonals.[10] The Russian page is more telling than the Italian, which is weakened by the name and address of the publishers printed in the left corner in an old-fashioned typeface, clashing with the stencil-like letters of the author's name and title. It is not certain that Ilia Zdanevich had seen this particular Italian publication but he was one of the first Russians with direct knowledge of Italian Futurist manifestos because his friend Lopatinsky had brought them from Paris to Tiflis in time for Zdanevich to take them to St Petersburg in 1911; the correspondence had continued[11] so he may well have received later publications from Europe from Lopatinsky through the post.

The Zdanevich family had close ties with Western Europe as the father taught French. It also seems likely that Ilia had some knowledge of Zurich Dada, for, as the American scholar, Gerald Janecek, has observed, the name of the hero of Zdanevich's play, *Ianko King of the Albanians (Ianko krul' albanskai)*,[12] sounds remarkably like the name of the Rumanian, Marcel Janco, who invented Dada in Zurich. Janecek finds further plausible connections, though his hypothesis that Zdanevich was in Zurich in 1916 seems most unlikely.[13] For whatever reasons, publications by 41° have a Dada spirit and, by 1923, Tabidze could say that Dadaism was already a reality in Georgia in 1918.[14] Moreover, when another play that Zdanevich wrote in Tiflis, *Le-Dantiu as a Beacon (lidantIU fAram)*, was published in Paris in 1923 it was accompanied by a booklet written by Georges Ribemont-Dessaignes who described 41° as the Russian form of literary Dada.[15]

A Dada – or, at the least, Expressionist – spirit is found in Moscow book design in the same years. The first book by Stepanova, *Gaust chaba*, made before Kruchenykh returned to Moscow, is already Dadaist: she produced fifty-four copies, writing the trans-sense words of her own poems boldly in ink across sheets of newspaper, folded so the lines of printing run at right angles to the handwritten lines; she added collage to some pages.[16] The idea of handwriting over printing had been used by Bobrov on his cover for *Lyre of Lyres* of 1917 [see 5], but the effect is different from Stepanova's book as he had used commercial printing to reproduce his design. Further examples of Stepanova's handmade books remain in her Moscow archive: they are single copies of exercise books

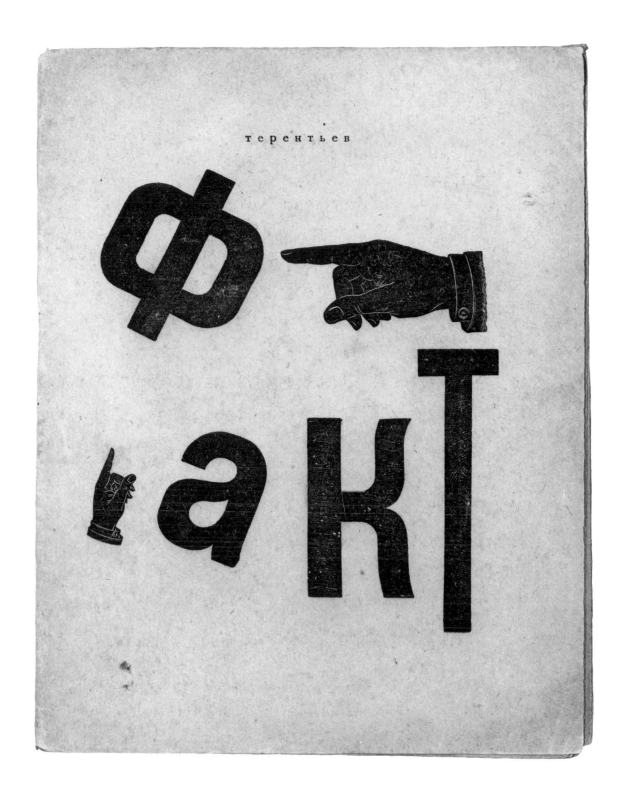

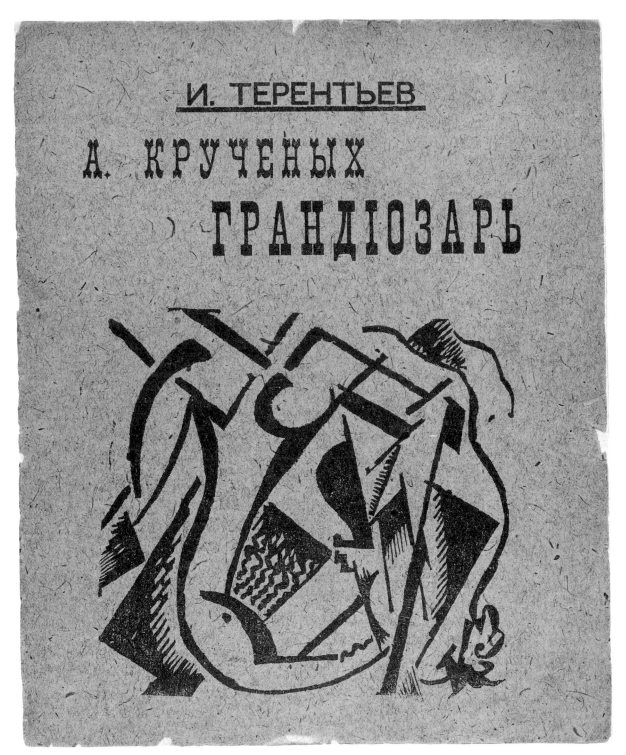

И. ТЕРЕНТЬЕВ

А. КРУЧЕНЫХ

ГРАНДІОЗАРЬ

38
I. Terentev, *Kruchenykh the Grandiozaire*, [1919] cover illustration by K. Zdanevich (C.185.a.13).

39 ▷
A. Kruchenykh, *Lacquered Tights*, 1919, cover by I. Zdanevich (C.114.m.23).

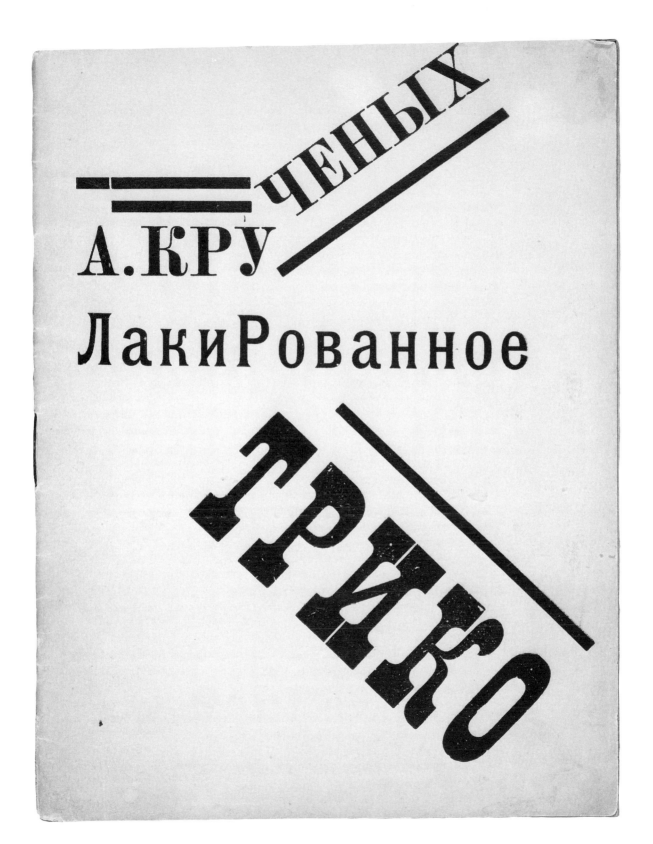

ЧЕНЫХ

А.КРУ

ЛакиРованное

ТРИКО

with poems typewritten and decorated with linear patterns, as well as pages of
abstract shapes painted in gouache, with words freely covering the white pages,
written in coloured, boldly informal letters.[17] Although some of the poems may be
Stepanova's own, others present a problem. The words of *Rtny khomle* and *Zigra ar*
(both untranslateable titles), are said to be by Kruchenykh, but the books are from
1918 and 1919 when he was living in the south and these titles do not appear in
Kruchenykh's listings of his own publications.[18] A plausible but unproveable
explanation is that Rozanova, whom Stepanova knew well before her death in
1918, gave her friend the texts; Kruchenykh may have sent them to Rozanova or
left the texts behind on his departure. At all events Stepanova continued to use
Dadaist lettering on posters for the Moscow exhibition '5 × 5 = 25' – held at the
Union of Poets in September 1921 – and even on the copies of the catalogues which
she decorated for the show.[19] Considering that the five artists took the occasion to
launch what they called 'Constructivist' graphics, Stepanova's work is
remarkably Dadaist; it is possible that the handmade methods were the result of
shortages of print or paper, or even money, but the painted lettering is far from
the theories of machine aesthetic which became the hallmark of Constructivist
graphics during the following year.

    The handmade character is still present in three book covers that
Rodchenko designed for Kruchenykh in 1922 after the latter had returned to
Moscow, sometime during the year before. To decorate the cover of *Transrational
(Zaum)* Rodchenko glued some of his own linocuts featuring geometric designs
and wrote the title by hand;[20] for the second book, *Transrationalists (Zaumniki)*,[21]
he made a linocut [plate 8], combining the straight line that he had discussed in a
theoretical text of 1921[22] with a style of lettering that he developed for film titling,
discussed below. For the third, *Tsotsa*, he made handwritten covers decorated
with coloured tissue paper [40], incorporating cut photographs as an element of
the collage on some copies.[23] Here the photographs were not yet made into
photomontage, which Rodchenko began to explore the same year, when he began
to work on the journal, *Cinema-Photo (Kino-fot)*.[24] In Moscow Kruchenykh himself
continued to use the typeface that had been used on the covers of books in Tiflis –
such as *Obesity of Roses* – on *Itchician (Zudesnik)*[25] and *Golodniak*.[26] The same
typeface was used for the covers of six books published in 1922 and 1923 by the
Moscow Association of Futurists (*MAF*) to which Kruchenykh contributed three
titles in the theory series;[27] the corresponding poets' series has two titles by
Mayakovsky and one by Aseev.[28] All the covers for the two series – printed at the
VKhUTEMAS – represent a regimented approach to design. They follow a
standardized pattern, with ruled horizontal and vertical lines marking
compartments [*see* 25]; a narrower margin on the left is used for wording repeated
on all the books, the wider area on the right side bearing the author's name and
the title of each volume. No designer is credited, but the division of space into
standardized units is an early use of a system illustrated by Gan some years later
[*see* 15] in the journal *Contemporary Architecture*. Kruchenykh evidently liked the
typeface, for it was used again several years later on Klutsis's cover [41] for
Kruchenykh's Alive! (Zhiv Kruchenykh!).[29]

    In the main, Kruchenykh retained a freer attitude than the
Constructivists to the design of covers for the books that he produced in Moscow.
He was well aware of alternatives because he took part in a meeting held to set up
the journal *LEF*[30] and contributed articles to its pages, but after Rodchenko began

41
B. Pasternak,
A. Kruchenykh and
others, *Kruchenykh's
Alive!*, 1925, cover by
G. Klutsis (C.114.m.26).

42 ▷
A. Kruchenykh, *Trans-
rational Language*, [1925]
cover by V. Kulagina
(C.114.m.25).

А. КРУЧЕНЫХ

ЗАУМНЫЙ ЯЗЫК

СЕЙФУЛЛИНОЙ

ВС. ИВАНОВА

ЛЕОНОВА

БАБЕЛЯ

А ВЕСЕЛОГО

designing *LEF* – for which he used regular hand-drawn letters in a strictly horizontal arrangement [*see* back cover] he designed no more books for Kruchenykh. Moreover, when other Constructivist artists such as Klutsis and his wife Valentina Kulagina worked with Kruchenykh, they conformed to his preference for a trans-rational approach. Like Rodchenko, Klutsis was capable of producing mechanical-looking letters, as he did for his cover for *The Furnace* [*see* 23b], yet when he designed the cover for *Kruchenykh's Alive!* he seems to have relished the slightly home-made quality of the printing. Kulagina designed a cover for Kruchenykh's book, *Transrational Language (Zaumnyi iazyk)*[31] which makes a good stylistic comparison with Rodchenko's design for Mayakovsky's poem, *Mayakovsky Smiles, Mayakovsky Laughs, Mayakovsky Jeers. (Maiakovskii ulybaetsia, Maiakovskii smeetsia, Maiakovskii izdevaetsia).*[32] She purposely made some of the title appear 'out of key' by allowing some letters to read out of register where the background colour changes from red to black [42], thus emphasizing their meaning. In contrast, Rodchenko strove to convey the greatest possible sense of order in his carefully spaced lettering overprinted with bands of green and red on the cover of Mayakovsky's poems [plate 9]. When Kulagina emulated this device on the right margin of her cover for Kruchenykh's *Lenin's Language (Iazyk Lenina)*[33] she forsook the precision of Rodchenko's overprinting, allowing her cover to retain a handmade quality. The reasons for this may, of course, be economic as well as aesthetic – Kruchenykh's books remain characterized by a small format and a short print run; he worked only on the margin of official recognition and many of his books were published by himself. Although some of them have cheaply printed covers, they preserve a distinct identity, including an occasional return to neo-primitivism [*see* 6]. Unlike Rodchenko's book covers, they are devoid of influence from the cinema and could not be confused with Western European designs.

Foreign connections have been mentioned several times in this study and should not be forgotten: Russian design is considered too often in isolation. Rodchenko's design for *Mayakovsky Smiles* is not unlike a publication in celebration of the fourth anniversary of the Bauhaus in Weimar in 1923, with typography by László Moholy-Nagy and layout by Herbert Bayer.[34] None the less the likeness is quite superficial, for, instead of printing sans-serif coloured letters – red and blue on black – like those on the cover of the Bauhaus book, Rodchenko achieved a remarkable effect simply by printing alternating bands of colour on the white cover so that his letters can be read where the unprinted paper shows through. He had used that device on *Transrationalists* [*see* plate 8] – discussed in the context of film below – and he used it for advertisements in 1923. His graphic work therefore has its own progression and any foreign influences were tempered by his own experience.

The link between Rodchenko's bookcovers and the advertisement posters that he began making with Mayakovsky in 1923 is close; title and design for the anthology *Flight (Let. Avio stikhi)*[35] are a reminder of their posters for the promotion of the Soviet aviation industry.[36] In spite of the apparent precision of Rodchenko's work, there are tiny aberrations in the careful arrangement for forms on the book cover [43] although they were produced with the aid of ruler and set squares. For instance, the margin of white round the red letter 'T' is interrupted by the wing of the aeroplane and the dot over the 'E' is out of register, but these are mere details in a carefully conceived and executed design. The

А. Крученых.

ОЖИРѢНIЕ РОЗ

А. КРУЧЕНЫХ

Г. ПЕТНИКОВ

В. ХЛЕБНИКОВ

ЗАУМНИКИ

1922

Plate 8
A. Kruchenykh,
V. Khlebnikov, G. Petnikov,
Transrationalists, 1922,
linocut cover by
A. Rodchenko (C.114.n.37).

Plate 9
V. V. Mayakovsky,
*Mayakovsky Smiles,
Mayakovsky Laughs,
Mayakovsky Jeers*, 1923,
cover by A. Rodchenko
(Cup.408.d.25).

И. ЭРЕНБУРГ

МАТЕРИАЛИЗАЦИЯ ФАНТАСТИКИ

КИНОПЕЧАТЬ

transition from handwritten covers such as *Tsotsa* [*see* 40] to work in a formal style took place when Rodchenko began work on *Cinema-Photo* with Gan, for whom he also designed the cover of the book, *Constructivism (Konstruktivizm).*[37] Through *Cinema-Photo* Rodchenko met the film producer, Dziga Vertov, and began work in film – creating inter-titles for Vertov's newsreels, *Film-Truth (Kino-pravda)*, which greatly influenced his work on books. His work with Vertov encouraged him to invent new ways with words – a propaganda approach of immediacy and clarity, enabling the semi-literate audience to grasp the key which the words provided to the moving pictures. As the films were topical the work had to be completed quickly: Rodchenko drew letters in black and white, sometimes making the titles appear in white on the black film, sometimes reversing the process, so that they appeared in black on a white background.[38] He also integrated the words instead of using them as a static element, which typically interrupts the flow of images in silent films.[39] The experience of working for cinema was paralleled in Rodchenko's book design: the cover of *Transrationalists* with its lino-cut letters handprinted so that the coloured paper shows through resembles his haphazard arrangement of letters on film inter-titles. The word 'Konstruktivizm' on the cover of Gan's book – which the author described as an 'Agitational book' – also looks like a film title except that, following Gan's theories of the need for Constructivists to work with industry, Rodchenko used more symmetrical letters, even though they are still handmade rather than chosen from the typographers' print-tray.

One of Gan's slogans in his book *Constructivism* – 'Painting cannot compete with photography'[40] – seems to have had an immediate effect on Russian book design. An early example is the cover which Popova designed in 1922 for *The Revolt of the Misanthropes*,[41] combining photography with typography [*see* plate 2]. The arrangement of letters is still surprisingly Dadaist – no concessions are made to the reader who must make sense of the illogical order. The underlying photograph of a gunner is, however, used in an unaltered state as though to replace a drawing or painting. It was Rodchenko, with his keen interest in cinema, who developed a radical way of 'editing' photographs much as Vertov cut and spliced the frames of his films. Vertov's newsreels broke new ground because of his editing techniques; characteristic of Russian avant-garde film in the early 1920s was the attention film directors gave to cutting. Instead of the four to five hundred cuts typical of Western film makers, they often used between one and four thousand.[42] The earliest illustrations which Rodchenko built up with photographs and text are his 'Psikhologiia' and 'Detektiv', published in *Cinema-Photo*,[43] but he developed the technique in covers for *LEF*, some of which seem closer to collage than photomontage. For the cover of *LEF* No.2 [*see* plate 1] Rodchenko combined photographs and pieces of text in an arrangement structured by ruled diagonals: in the triangles at each side he tipped the photographs towards the centre, creating a vertiginous effect more like Vertov's film montage than conventional perspective.

Rodchenko quickly mastered the art of cutting still photographs and combining unlikely images in unusual spatial arrangements. The apogee of this technique is the set of photomontage illustrations that he made for Mayakovsky's poem *About This (Pro eto)*[44] of 1923. This love poem, dedicated 'To her and to me', was the vehicle of the poet's feelings during two months of separation agreed between himself and his love, Lily Brik, from December 1921 to February 1922.

After the introduction to his poem, Mayakovsky entitled the first section 'The Ballad of Reading Gaol', taking the title from Oscar Wilde's poem, which had recently been translated into Russian.[45] Wilde's modern epic, based on a traditional folk form, is divided into six parts with lilting verses and simple but telling language; it must have appealed to Mayakovsky in his search for a post-Revolutionary form, and its refrain, 'And all men kill the thing they love', no doubt struck him as appropriate to his own situation of hopeless love. He thought of his flat as his own jail – albeit from choice and with the telephone and postal service as a means of communication with the outside world. His tormented feelings are captured by Rodchenko in montages formed from photographs taken by other people[46] of commonplace objects – including telephones and animals – as well as of the poet and his love, which he arranged freely within the allotted rectangular space. Running through the poem are the twin ideas of Mayakovsky as a polar bear, recently encountered with Lily in the Berlin Zoo, and of impending suicide; Rodchenko combined these in a masterly montage [44] of bears and icebergs with the poet standing pensively on a bridge, where ironwork appears to rear up in front of him, doubling as bridges and the head of an iron bedstead. These sections of ironwork bridges seem also to parody constructions by contemporary artists such as those by Popova and Aleksandr Vesnin for the stage [see 64] as well as poems by Gastev mentioned in the Introduction.

From the cover of *About This* [45] Lily Brik stares intently at the reader as though from a poster of a silent-film star – a role which she had indeed played with Mayakovsky in 1918.[47] Shklovsky has drawn attention to the dependence of the poem on contemporary film: 'Neither can the poem "About this" – whose hero passes from one circle to another and undergoes various metamorphoses – be understood without a knowledge of the cinematography of the time, without the awareness of what it meant then for artists to be violently confronted with fragments endowed with a unified overall sense ...'.[48] Mayakovsky's interest was sustained during the 1920s when he wrote scenarios for a number of films;[49] Rodchenko's fascination with film continued to inspire many of his book covers, including a scheme capable of variation for a series of popular detective stories – *Mess Mend or the Yankee in Petrograd (Mess Mend ili Ianki v Petrograde)* – written by Marietta Shaginian under the pseudonym Jim Dollar.[50] For all ten volumes Rodchenko devised a complicated geometric layout combining colour with black and white, by dividing the cover into alternating coloured and black fields carrying white lettering. The central areas vary from cover to cover: they include cleverly cut photographs, including close-ups, reflecting the description to be found on the title page of volume one: 'cinematographic novel'. He chose a different colour for each cover [46] and the series, which came out in 1924, remains most effective, though cheaply produced.

Photography could also be used for documentary purposes and soon new ideas transformed the appearance of periodicals. The organ of the Trade Unions *Labour Herald (Vestnik truda)*[51] broke with its undistinguished typographic design by placing enlarged cut-out photographs of two delegates in front of graphic devices on the cover of the first number of 1925 [47]. Inside there are sixteen montages, some signed by the artists Klutsis and Sergei Senkin, another five unattributed. It was the only number of the journal to be illustrated in this novel way and it is possible that readers missed conventionally posed photographs of groups of delegates sitting or standing in rows (the issue records

44

V. Mayakovsky, *About This*,
1923, opposite p.16:
illustration by
A. Rodchenko (C.131.k.12).

45

V. Mayakovsky, *About This*,
1923, cover by
A. Rodchenko, with
photograph of Lily Brik
(C.131.k.12).

Я уши лаплю —
напрасные мнешь!
слышу
мой
мой собственный голос
мне лапы дырявит голоса нож.

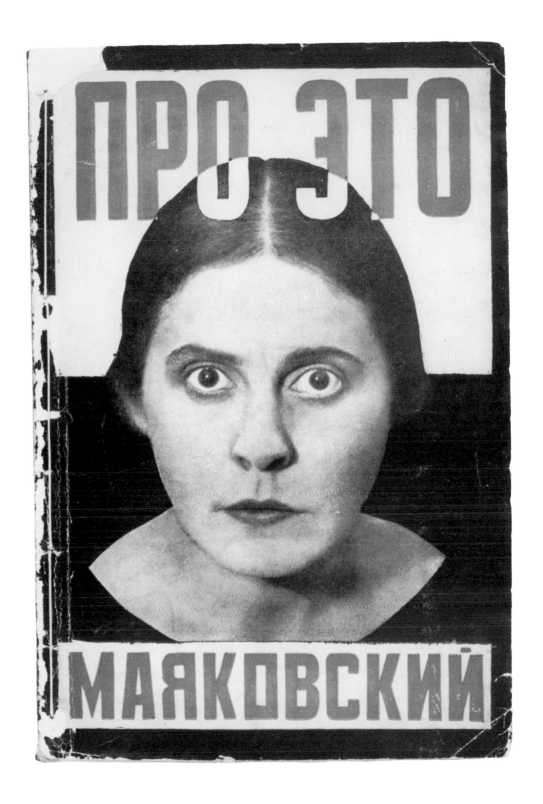

46
Jim Dollar (pseud), *Mess
Mend or The Yankee in
Petrograd*, 1924, Vol.1, *Mask
of Vengeance* and Vol.7, *The
Black Hand*, 1924, covers
by A. Rodchenko
(C.185.a.32).

47
Labour Herald, No.1 1925,
unsigned cover, by
G. Klutsis, S. Senkin or
another, unidentified
(PP.1423.phk).

a Union conference), especially as individual faces are more difficult to recognize in wittily composed photomontages. The year before the same artists had designed the cover [48] of *Tomorrow (Zavtra)*,[52] by the young Communist writer, Iury Libedinsky, and provided eight photomontage illustrations for the novel. This type of illustration was topical that year, for the same publishers, the Communist Young Guard (*Molodaia gvardiia*), commissioned the same artists to illustrate *Children and Lenin (Deti i Lenin)*, for which they cut and pasted photographs of groups and individuals and combined them with arrows and bands to form a new type of image.[53]

Lenin had been enthusiastic about the propaganda value of photography: both cinema and photography had been nationalized in 1919 and, in his instructions to *Narkompros* in January 1922, he said: 'You must not only show films, but also interesting photographs with explanatory notes for propaganda.'[54] Over the next years Russians developed photomontage in a manner that differs from European examples, largely because the Russian form was so closely connected with film and theatre. A telling comparison was printed in *LEF* No.4, where a photomontage by Paul Citroën (then working at the Bauhaus) was printed beside a Russian example – a montage by Popova for Meyerhold's production of *The Earth in Turmoil (Zemlia dybom)* – with a short article on the technique.[55] Citroën's photographic views of city buildings are packed side by side to exclude any background, but Popova's design was not a true photomontage, since her

48

Iu. Libedinsky, *Tomorrow*,
1924, cover by S. Senkin
(12840.k.16).

49

V. Mayakovsky, *A
Conversation with a Tax
Inspector about Poetry*,
1926, back cover by
A. Rodchenko (not British
Library copy).

50

V. Mayakovsky, *A
Conversation with a Tax
Inspector about Poetry*,
1926, opp.p.14, 'and try to
write them yourselves'
illustration by
A. Rodchenko (C.136.b.34).

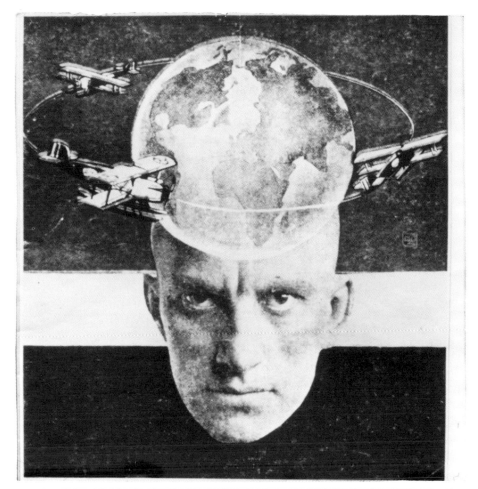

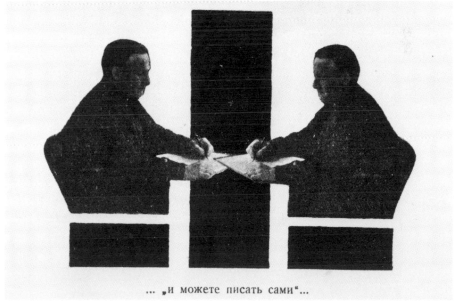

... „и можете писать сами"...

images are glued to a plywood background with superimposed lettering.[56] Hers is a new type of picture, with its antecedents in Suprematism, where coloured abstract forms are arranged on a plain background [see plate 15].

Rodchenko's photographic inspiration continued to the end of the 1920s, often in fruitful partnership with Mayakovsky. On the back cover [49] of *A Conversation with a Tax Inspector about Poetry (Razgovor s fininspektorom o poezii)*[57] – which Mayakovsky based on his correspondence with such an official – Rodchenko did not bother with the hackneyed imagery which he could have extracted from the lines ' "Was your journey necessary?" … what if during these last fifteen years I've ridden to death a dozen Pegasuses?!' but used the words 'All poetry is a journey into the unknown', to imagine Mayakovsky's head (represented by a photograph) as a world in itself, circled by aeroplanes. At the same time he presented the reader with a prosaic montage [50] directly illustrating Mayakovsky's concluding lines, inviting the disbelieving tax inspector to have a go at poetry-writing himself: 'Why here then, comrades, take my own quill, and try to write them yourselves.'[58] Rodchenko also began to play more serious 'games' with photography. For the cover of Mayakovsky's poem, dramatically named *Syphilis (Sifilis)* [51],[59] he printed a woman's head in negative and continued the metaphor in the photographic illustrations. For instance, opposite page ten, a small man – printed positively – raises his hat to the woman's head – seen in close-up and printed in negative – which dominates the page [52]. On his cover for Erenburg's *Materialization of the Fantastic (Materializatsiia fantastiki)*[60] Rodchenko used the same cover photograph as he had for *Syphilis*, but printed it in alternating vertical strips of positive and negative [plate 10]. The superlative quality of the printing shows up the poor quality of the earlier *Syphilis* which had been printed in Tiflis.[61] No doubt this is because the publisher of Erenburg's theoretical discussion about film was Film-press *(Kino-pechat')*, which evidently had access to superior equipment.

Rodchenko's photographic experiments were rivalled by those of Lissitzky, whose originality lay, however, not in manipulating the printing of existing negatives, but in manipulating the process at an earlier stage, often by superimposing negatives and making a print from them. Thus his cover [53] for Selvinsky's *Notes of a Poet (Zapiski poeta)* of 1928[62] is a portrait of the artist, Jean Arp, which he had composed in Switzerland. He had superimposed the two exposures of the artist's head on a copy of the Dada periodical *391*, choosing an issue, of March 1920, which had the number '391' repeated, so it appears to echo the double portrait in the resulting print.[63] For the book cover Lissitzky arranged the author's name and the title over the photograph, adding the name of the hero – Evgeny Nei – to Arp's collar. He evidently failed to find room for the words 'State Publishing House' and placed them instead of the title along the spine; this has the effect of reinforcing the satirical character of the book, Selvinsky's 'autobiography' of the poet Evgeny Nei, with its theme of the poet's conscience, expressing his goals and doubts in a new, socialist epoch.[64]

Lissitzky's cover [see plate 16] of a book on students' architectural projects produced at *VKhUTEMAS (Arkhitektura. Raboty Arhitekturnogo fakul'teta Vkhutemasa 1920-1927)*[65] is likewise based on an earlier invention of his own. In this case he added lettering to the photograph of his own hand holding compasses over graph paper, which he had used in a composite self-portrait of 1924.[66] His technique of combining two or more negatives by laying them on a

привинтило винтом.
Слепующий
через недели!
Как дождаться
с голодным ртом.
—Забыл,
разлюбил,
забросил Том
С белой
рогожу
делит!—
Не заработать ей
и не скрасть.
Везде
полисмены пол зонтиком.
А мистеру Свифту
последнюю страсть
раздула
эта экзотика.
Потело
тело
под бельецом
от черненького мясца.
Он тыкал
доллары
в руку, в лицо
в голодные месяца.

10

sheet of bromide paper was analogous to that of placing an object directly on
light-sensitive paper invented by the American Surrealist artist, Man Ray, which
Lissitzky also used.[67] Although he used such techniques rarely after he left
Switzerland in 1925, he advocated the process in an article published in the
journal, *Soviet Photo (Sovetskoe foto)* in 1929.[68] Having dismissed photography (and
cinema) as a mirror of the new world in 1922,[69] he had come to recognize its
potential as a new form of art with properties not available to painting so he
argued for an extension of camera-less photography, using light and materials in
a creative way, which he termed 'photo-painting' (*fotopis'*) and the result can be
seen in covers he made for a series of architectural books produced in Vienna in
1930.[70]

　　　　While Lissitzky made a great contribution to publications by his
creative use of photography, he is equally remembered for rethinking the concept
of the printed book. The sheer invention of his design of Mayakovsky's poems, *For
the Voice (Dlia golosa)*,[71] of 1923 – with its page margins stepped like an address
book to form an index to the poems [54] – equals that of Rodchenko's design for
About This of the same year. Each approached his task in a different way:
Rodchenko was already applying ideas that he had learned from working with
film to his photomontage illustrations, whereas Lissitzky had not by then
discovered the camera as a creative tool. He built his illustrations from the
printers' stock, printing in red as well as black to enliven the pages. The design
owes a debt to his Proun paintings, still present in residual form in the
frontispiece photograph of 'The Announcer' borrowed from the lithographs of

53
I. Selvinsky, *Notes of a Poet*,
1928, cover by El Lissitsky
(Cup.410.f.69).

54
V. Mayakovsky, *For the Voice*, 1923, double page showing illustration to the poem 'Left March' and index system on right, both designed by El Lissitzky (C.114.mm.33).

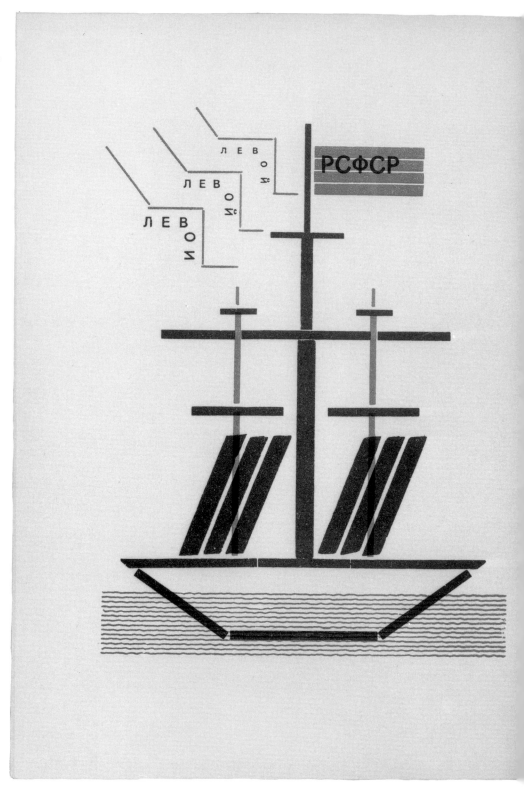

ЛЕВЫЙ МАРШ

МАТРОСАМ

Разворачивайтесь в марше!
Словесной не место кляузе.
Тише, ораторы!

МАРШ

НАШ МАРШ

МОЙ МАЙ

СВОЛОЧИ

ИНТЕР-
НАЦИОНАЛ

АРМИИ
ИСКУССТВ

ПРИКАЗ № 2

А ВЫ

КАДЕТ

КУМА

ЛЮБОВЬ

К ЛОШАДЯМ

СОЛНЦЕ

'electro-mechanical puppets' which he had made for the opera *Victory over the Sun*.[72] Proun art works had, however, been created mainly from the geometer's vocabulary and were 'non-objective'; for Mayakovsky's revolutionary poems Lissitzky reintroduced an element of narrative by creating recognizable objects. For instance, he created a boat from the printers' straight rules and wavy lines [54] to illustrate 'Left March' for the Red Marines: 'Rally the ranks into a march!/Now's no time to quibble or browse there./Silence you orators!' The artist rationalized the originality of the book thus:

> *The book is created with the resources of the compositor's type case alone. The possibilities of two-colour printing (overlap, cross hatching and so on) have been exploited to the full. My pages stand in much the same relation to the poems as an accompanying piano to a violin. Just as the poet in his poem unites concept and sound, I have tried to create an equivalent unity using the poem and typography.*[73]

For the Voice was published by the branch of the Soviet Russian State Publishing House in Berlin and the technical proficiency of the printed illustrations was linked with the excellence of German technology, unmatched at the time in Russia. Yet the book can be criticized for the undistinguished traditional typography of pages of unillustrated text which Lissitzky was rather proud of having left to a German typesetter who knew no Russian. They are, however, typical of the internal pages of most books with Constructivist book covers and title-pages, where the rest of the text is often unremarkable. A good example of this – also from Berlin – is *A Petersburg Tale (Povest' Peterburgskaia)* by Boris Pilniak, where the cover and contents are in a conventional style and only the title-page [55] is a novelty.[74] The book is dated 1922 and the design was truly avant-garde, not only for the decorative use of abstract forms but for the variety of typography. Conventional illustrations in the book are by Vasily Masiutin so, if he designed the title-page, he must carefully have studied Lissitzky's designs, the closest parallel being the cover [56] for the journal *Epopee (Epopeia)*.[75] Here Lissitzky built two types of cyrillic 'e' from the same components; he repeated the letter 'p', using three simple 'bricks' for the first and emphasizing the second by outlining it with black lines and creating a solid centre from a black square. The same device is used for the 'P' of 'Pilniak' on the title-page. It is tempting to surmise that Lissitzky made the design, though it is generally more fussy than his own, and Masiutin was capable of the outstanding design for Blok's *The Twelve (Dvenadtsat')* [see 9].[76]

The 'o', which is given a prominent position on the cover of *Epopee*, recurs on the cover of *For the Voice* [57] where it serves no purpose as a letter, but simply balances three abstract forms. It looks back to an anonymous cover [58] for Mayakovsky's poem, *Man. Thing*[77] published in Moscow in 1918. There the enlarged letter 'o' serves to link the author's name and *Chelovek* (Man) in much the same way as words are linked in acrostics and crossword puzzles. Lissitzky found the device useful: the letter 'Ia' in 'Dlia' on the cover of *For the Voice (Dlia golosa)* is read horizontally in Mayakovsky's name and vertically at the end of 'dlia'. Here there is an unexpected twist – Lissitzky turned the letters of the word 'golosa' sideways to ensure that they are read as a separate word. In the same way he had already designed a typeset cover for *Vladimir Mayakovsky, 'Mystery' or 'Buffo' (Vladimir Maiakovskii, 'Mysteriia' ili 'Buff')*[78] where, unable to find a pattern with the given letters, he had used the entire cyrillic alphabet printed vertically

КАРЛО ГОЦЦИ

ТУРАНДОТ

ПРИНЦЕССА

1923

ТРЕТЬЯ СТУДИЯ М.Х.Т.
ИМЕНИ ЕВГ. ВАХТАНГОВА

down the centre as a decorative feature, allowing the title words to pick up the correct letter where it fell in the alphabet and so dictate the position of the horizontal words of which they form an element [59]. This arrangement depends on ingenuity as well as chance; Lissitzky imposed his own order by varying the typesize of author and title, which he had to reduce to the single word 'Maiakovskii' for the scheme to work.

At the same time Lissitsky was working in the international field, designing covers for journals in Germany, Austria, Holland, Yugoslavia, and even New York.[79] This put him in touch with a very wide range of publications and a variety of designers and he found no difficulty in working imaginatively alongside them. He became more adept at using the resources of mechanical printing which were more advanced in the West than in Russia. When he returned to his homeland in 1925 and began to take responsibility for the design of exhibitions as well as their catalogues, he invented more ways of using print.[80] Although he was never concerned with foreign publications, Rodchenko also had the chance to travel, as a member of the Soviet delegation to Paris in 1925, but he returned to Russia convinced that the Communist system was the best. A major difference in the work of these two major exponents of book design is Rodchenko's respect for the intrinsic two-dimensional nature of a page and Lissitzky's daring disregard for it. This is particularly obvious in a comparison of Lissitzky's design for *Object* [60] where the dynamic organism seems to set the whole cover in motion, and Rodchenko's title page for *LEF* [see 86] where the integrity of the horizontal position expected in all printed alphabets is rigidly observed. The method for this type of construction was explained in an article and diagram [see 15] in *SA* No.2, 1926. The scheme served equally for composing advertisements and book covers, and, on the latter, Rodchenko sometimes used an all-over grid as a decorative device. In 1924 he used one as the basis for *Altogether. Verses* [see 32], floating the letters over the top of the grid instead of using it in an obvious way to provide anchorage for the letters. He gave the back cover equal importance, often carrying the design across the spine, so the spine causes no break between front and back. This is particularly obvious in the design for *All's Well on the Street* [see 31] where the whole area is divided into 'windows' of varying sizes with some filled-in with dense grids. Again the lettering is floated over the spaces, and some of the words are overlapped; Rodchenko overprinted blue on red to create density in the centre panel. His grids seem marginally to parody those of Mondrian, but this may be a coincidence, for he was equally at home making an elaborate pattern from diagonals and lozenges in a cover for Tretiakov's poems, *Vocalist. Verses (Rechevik. Stikhi)*.[81] Rodchenko increasingly initialled his cover designs, possibly because other designers were copying his style. Certainly it is difficult to know whether Rodchenko or an imitator was responsible for the cover of *Literature of Fact* [see 30], another design based on a grid system, carried out in green and black. By the end of the 1920s Constructivist typographic design must have seemed as much a style to be emulated as a way of working, with its own rationale. The design of commercial editions flowered in Soviet Russia during the 1920s and is of even wider interest today than it was at the time of its invention.

55
B. Pilniak, *A Petersburg
Tale*, 1922, title-page by
V. Masiutin (012590.c.21).

56 ▷
Epopee, No.2, 1922, cover
by El Lissitzky
(PP.4842.dcb).

ЭПО-
ПЕЯ.
ЛИТЕРАТУРНЫЙ ЕЖЕМѢСЯЧНИКЪ

№ 2
ПОДЪ РЕДАКЦIЕЙ:

1922
СЕНТЯБРЬ

АНДРЕЯ
БѢЛАГО

57
V. Mayakovsky, *For the Voice*, 1923, cover by El Lissitzky (C.114.mm.33).

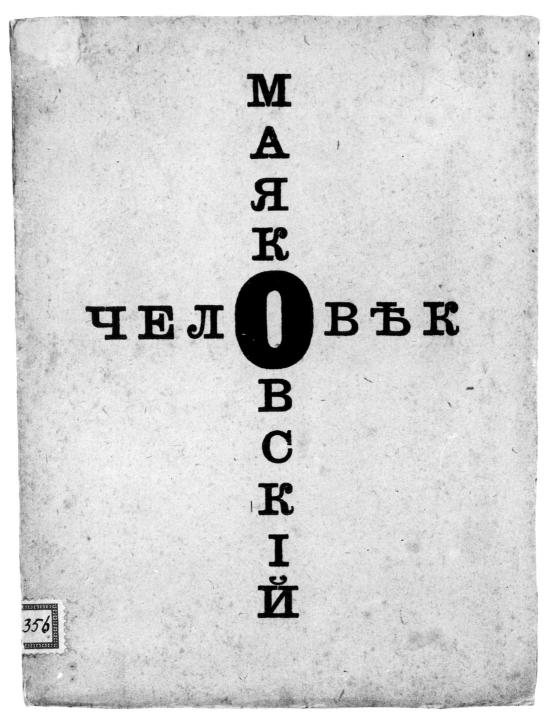

58
V. Mayakovsky, *Man,
Thing* [1918] cover,
designer unidentified
(C.114.mm.11).

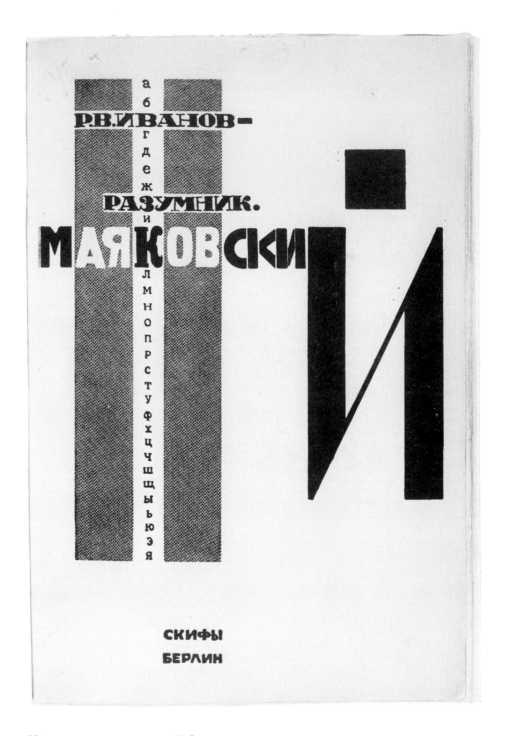

59
Ivanov-Razumnik,
Vladimir Mayakovsky,
'Mystery' or 'Buffo', 1922,
cover by El Lissitzky
(Cup.410.f.72).

60 ▷
Object, No.3, 1922, cover by
El Lissitzky (Cup.408.g.25).

BERLIN 1922

OBJET

ВЕЩЬ

3

REVUE INTERNATIONALE DE L'ART MODERNE МЕЖДУНАРОДНОЕ ОБОЗРЕНИЕ СОВРЕМЕННОГО ИСКУССТВА INTERNATIONALE RUNDSCHAU DER KUNST DER GEGENWART

GEGENSTAND

Theatre: a revolution in design

Revolutions in Russian theatre – in production, in play writing, and, above all, in scenic design – pre-date the political changes of 1917; the years following political revolution saw radical developments from these rich antecedents. A steady progression of directors had emerged in Moscow and Petersburg following the founding of the Moscow Arts Theatre at the turn of the century by Konstantin Stanislavsky and Nemirovich-Danchenko. Sergei Diaghilev's flamboyant World of Art (*Mir iskusstva*) ballet and opera productions are the ones best known in the West because, although prepared in St Petersburg, they were shown in Paris. But, by 1917, equally remarkable productions had been staged in Moscow and Petrograd. Nikolai Evreinov had experimented with re-creations of medieval mystery plays in his Old-Time Theatre; Aleksandr Tairov had established his Moscow Chamber (*Kamernyi*) Theatre with its emphasis on mime, stage-lighting reform and settings by Futurist artists; Vsevolod Meyerhold had developed two distinct production styles, one lavish and conventional for the Imperial theatres and another, radical and inventive for his Studio Theatre. By choice all these directors worked as partners with invited artists who designed sets and costumes. It was usual for these artists to submit theatre designs to art exhibitions alongside their easel paintings and drawings.

The political revolutions of 1917 interrupted the work of these directors very little; productions took place within a few weeks of the October Revolution. However, Diaghilev, who was already in Western Europe, remained in exile thereafter. The abolition of censorship for a short time allowed Tairov to produce Oscar Wilde's previously banned play, *Salome*, in Moscow in 1917. Many theatres at first continued with their pre-Revolutionary repertoire but theatre was soon recognized as such an important tool for propaganda that even the classics seemed to require a new approach, and the 1920s was a decade of unprecedented theatrical innovation. Many books were devoted to theatre and, by 1930, a comprehensive study of Russian theatre design by Joseph Gregor and René Fülöp-Miller had been published in German and English editions: the profusely illustrated book remains one of the best sources for production photographs.[1]

The covers of many Russian plays and books on theatre reflect the tenor of theatrical invention. For instance, the cover [61] of Evreinov's *Theatrical Innovations (Teatral'nye novatsii)*[2] with its design of stylized masks signed with the initials *'PAK'*, conveys the conservatism of that director's style which, by 1922,

61
N. Evreinov, *Theatrical Innovations*, [1922], cover, initialled 'PAK' (011840.m.64).

ЕВРЕИНОВ

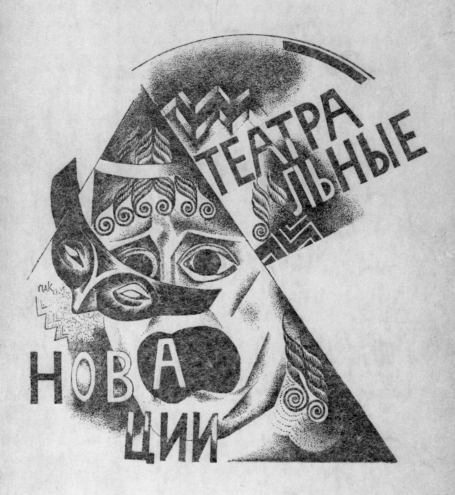

ТЕАТРА ЛЬНЫЕ НОВАЦИИ

КНИГОИЗДАТЕЛЬСТВО
"ТРЕТЬЯ СТРАЖА"

62

A. Tairov, *Notes of a Director*, [1921] p.7: illustration by A. Ekster for section inscribed 'Director' (C.114.1.4).

lacked the radical approach of Tairov and Meyerhold and even of Stanislavsky's gifted pupil, Sergei Vakhtangov. In 1923 a commemorative volume was devoted to Vakhtangov's colourful production of Carlo Gozzi's *Princess Turandot (Printsessa Turandot)*[3] for the Third Studio of the Moscow Arts Theatre. Unfortunately he died of illness without seeing this production, which he directed from his hospital bed. Costumes and decor were by Ignaty Nivinsky who was also responsible for the book, providing a cubistic design for the cover, printed in pastel shades of yellow, blue, pink and green [plate 11]. The publication, which includes colour plates as well as photographs, gives an idea of the look of the production, but cannot convey its calculated spontaneity. The theatre seated only three hundred people, providing an intimate space which Vakhtangov exploited. He first introduced the members of the cast to the audience by letting them take a bow in front of the curtain, wearing formal evening dress. As the curtain rose the actors proceeded to prepare for the spectacle by transforming first their clothes and then the stage with pieces of coloured material, moving rhythmically in time to music until they had created an illusion of China. The director thus encouraged the audience to share the preparations for the fairy story, and he prevented them from losing themselves entirely in the spectacle by having the actors get in and out of character several times during the performance. *Princess Turandot* proved so attractive to audiences that it ran to over a thousand performances and was successfully revived in the 1970s, when it played for several years.[4]

Numerous books on a less lavish scale provide information about Tairov's Kamerny Theatre. Thus, in 1922 a first book on 'Theatrical matters', published by the Russian Theatre Union, was devoted to Tairov's theatre, (*Vremennik Kamernogo teatra*),[5] and, as late as 1934, when the opportunity for theatrical invention was already curtailed by increased censorship, a book illustrating twenty years of the Kamerny Theatre and its artists was published by the All-Russian Theatre Union.[6] The Kamerny Theatre itself regularly published books and journals, usually designed by the same avant-garde artists who designed its productions; their covers give an indication of the style which Tairov favoured at that moment. Sometimes the appearance of a book may be misleading: for instance, that of Iakov Apushkin's *The Kamerny Theatre (Kamernyi teatr)*[7] of 1927, which included many production photographs as well as a signed photograph of Tairov himself. The cover design by the two Stenberg brothers, Georgy and Vladimir, may suggest a Suprematist style because of its four superimposed squares of diminishing sizes on an orange background. However, Tairov never favoured Suprematism and the Stenbergs were Constructivists: their cover design of a large white square, overlapped in turn by a light grey, a dark grey, and finally, a black one represents the basic forms which served as raw material for constructing the new scenic mode which Tairov had described in his 1921 *Notes of a Director (Zapiski rezhissera)*.[8]

The cover and vignettes of Tairov's *Notes of a Director* [62] were drawn by Aleksandra Ekster in a strongly Expressionist vein, echoing this artist's designs for the Kamerny's most recent production, Shakespeare's *Romeo and Juliet* – a spectacular event of 1921. Some of Ekster's designs are reproduced in a 1922 monograph, *Aleksandra Ekster*, quickly translated into English and French.[9] It was written by the critic Iakov Tugendkhold, who devoted more of his text to her work in the theatre than to her easel painting. After designing the curtains for the stage of the Kamerny Theatre in 1914 Ekster had gone on to work closely with

Tairov on several notable productions; in each case she was able to subordinate her own ideas to his overall conception. The partnership resulted in the first use in Russia of a cyclorama for *Thamira the Lyrist (Famira Kifared)* in 1916;[10] the pioneering use of a raked stage in *Salome* (1917), and a multi-level setting for *Romeo and Juliet* four years later. In comparison with *Notes of a Director*, the cover of the Russian edition of *Aleksandra Ekster* is remarkably restrained: her name is simply printed in red capitals on a grey textured card.[11] However, when Tairov's *Notes of a Director* was published in German translation (*Das entfesselte Theater*)[12] the cover was designed by a new artist in a different style. It appeared in 1923 with an innovative design in Constructivist vein by Lissitzky, following the visit of the Kamerny Theatre to Berlin in autumn 1922.

Who, What, When in the Kamerny Theatre 1914-1924 (Kto, chto, kogda v Moskovskom Kamernom teatre 1914-1924),[13] designed two years later by Georgy Stenberg [63], is another example of Constructivist book design, though the cover does not have quite the same *élan* as Lissitzky's. Inside the book, there are pages devoted to production photographs of the set for G. K. Chesterton's *The Man who was Thursday* designed by the architect/painter, Aleksandr Vesnin. These show Tairov's new preference for Constructivist stage design taken to the extreme of replacing conventional scenery by a free-standing multi-level structure. Although the play was not put on until 1923, Vesnin had designed the set the year before, so it bears comparison with a structure which his friend and colleague, Popova, had made for a production by Meyerhold. Both artists conceived their stage designs in three-dimensional, free-standing form, more like stage architecture than previous multi-level stage scenery (such as Ekster's for *Romeo and Juliet*). The differences between Popova and Vesnin's approach are particularly noticeable in the two surviving maquettes where it is obvious that Popova's large wooden apparatus closely resembles the windmill in which the action of Crommelynk's play, *The Magnanimous Cuckold*, took place, whereas Vesnin's multi-level construction [64] represents a view of a modern city, complete with moving pavements and elevators to carry the actors from one place to another, as required by G. K. Chesterton's detective story.[14] Moreover, the two sets looked quite unalike on the stage because of the difference in the approach of the two directors. Production photographs show Vesnin's construction partially hidden behind the traditional proscenium arch which Tairov retained to separate the stage action from his audience; Meyerhold tried to bridge the gap between audience and stage by stripping a Moscow stage of its illusionistic backdrops and flats and replacing them with Popova's stark 'machinery for acting', enlivened by very few realistic props.[15] Although Vesnin had worked for Tairov before, the proposal by Vesnin and Popova for the staging of a multi-media entertainment on Khodynskoe Field had led to the invitation for Popova to work with Meyerhold. For the Third Congress of the Comintern the two artists had imagined model cities – of Capitalism and of the Future – linked by a network of cables carrying slogans held in the air by airships. Unrealizable in 1921, this fantasy served as a trail-blazer for architecture as well as theatre design.[16]

As has been mentioned in Chapter 1, Meyerhold had answered Lunacharsky's call to people working in the cultural arena to support the Bolshevik regime and, in 1918, had joined the Communist Party. He thought that theatre should play a political role in establishing and extending the new government and believed that new audiences – largely made up of Red Army

КТО ЧТО КОГДА в КАМЕРНОМ ТЕАТРЕ 1914 X 1924

ОМКТ

soldiers and factory workers who were given free seats – would respond to more
vigorous production styles than those which traditional bourgeois audiences
were used to. For him the proscenium arch, seen as a 'fourth wall' or 'window'
onto a fictitious stage world, was no longer appropriate in post-Revolutionary
times. Production ideas inspired by the Japanese *Kabuki* theatre and Italian
Commedia dell'arte which he had developed in his Petrograd Studio Theatre before
1917[17] served as a basis for his new style. He was an early adherent of
Constructivism in its aim to break down barriers between art and everyday life,
and he extended Constructivist art onto the stage, particularly using 'mechanical'
scenery, which his actors could use for climbing and clowning. He had long since
rejected the psychological approach used in Stanislavsky's Moscow Arts Theatre
and, for productions such as *The Magnanimous Cuckold*, he now developed a
physical style of acting that demanded actors train like athletes or circus artistes,
with a series of exercises which he named biomechanics. Unlike Tairov,
Meyerhold did not produce a stream of illustrated books as advertisements or
mementoes of his productions, though he wrote numerous articles. In one of
them, entitled 'The actor of the future' (*Aktor budushchego*), he reviewed Tairov's
Notes of a Director for the journal, *Press and Revolution (Pechat' i revoliutsiia)*,
contrasting what he called the 'studied balleticism' of the Kamerny theatre with

Plate 13
V.V.Mayakovsky, *The Bed Bug*, 1929, cover by
A. Rodchenko (C.133.b.18).

his own acting system based on American Taylorism, which he believed would achieve maximum productivity for the actor, just as it had for the industrial worker.[18] A book about his theatre was published in 1925[19] but, in spite of Meyerhold's closeness to Constructivist artists, its design is far less interesting than books about the Kamerny Theatre. Meyerhold was close to the *LEF* group, and a good photograph of Popova's montage for the decor of his 1923 production of *The Earth Rampant* – sometimes translated as *Earth in Turmoil (Zemlia dybom)* – was reproduced in the journal *LEF* in 1924.[20] *The Earth Rampant* was conceived as a multi-media production and actors riding motorbikes and driving a lorry carrying the coffin of a martyred Red Army soldier roared up the aisles between the rows of spectators in his Moscow production designed by Popova. A connection with film was provided by a screen hung from the central 'machine for acting' – a crane – on which slogans were flashed during the performance to signal the theme of each episode; by indicating the end of the scenes, they replaced the drop curtain.[21] The play had been rewritten by Tretiakov from an original verse-play, *La Nuit*, by the French Communist writer, Marcel Martinet, which the Russian transformed with allusions to recent history, rewriting the dialogue in a propaganda style. When an open-air production was mounted in 1924 for an audience of twenty-five thousand at the Fifth Congress of the Comintern in Moscow, Tretiakov changed the original ending from tragedy to triumph.

Although publicly acclaimed, such productions were not always appreciated by officialdom. However, a greater problem for the regime was the lack of playwrights dedicated to Bolshevism. For the first anniversary of the October Revolution, Mayakovsky responded to a call for new plays with *Mystery-Bouffe (Misteriia-Buff)*, which he described in the sub-title as an 'Heroic, epic and satirical creation of our time in three acts with five scenes'.[22] It proved extremely difficult to recruit actors and to find a theatre willing to put on the play, even though the production was supported by Lunacharsky himself. Eventually three performances by student actors were fitted into the programme of the Petrograd Conservatoire, though the bookshop there refused to sell the text. The cover for the book was adapted from the poster that showed a globe with outlined continents – Asia, Africa, Australia and Europe; these were entitled 'old world' (*staryi svet*) and firmly crossed-out with red lines;[23] the symbolism is more condensed on the book cover [plate 12] where the schematic globe is crossed out by Mayakovsky's name and the title in hand-written script. The stylized sets were designed by Malevich, and his huge blue 'globe' for the first act must have reminded some viewers of the abstract designs which he had made for Kruchenykh's opera *Victory over the Sun (Pobeda nad solntsem)* when it was given in 1913 in St Petersburg.[24] However, unlike that Futurist theatre production by the writers and artists themselves, *Mystery-Bouffe* was directed by Meyerhold, who welcomed Mayakovsky's modern mystery play. Mayakovsky had begun to write the play in August 1917 – before the October Revolution – and it is perhaps surprising that Lunacharsky encouraged its production because the text was politically extremely naive. The characters were divided into two camps – the 'clean' and the 'unclean' – the latter represented the workers, the former the bourgeoisie. The first act took place in an Ark, from which the bourgeoisie threw out the workers; after visiting 'Hell' and 'Paradise' they ended up in a 'Promised Land' which was the world of the first act transformed by Revolution. The play achieved some success with the public and Mayakovsky hoped for another

В. МАЯКОВСКИЙ

КЛОП

ГОСУДАРСТВЕННОЕ ИЗДАТЕЛЬСТВО
1929

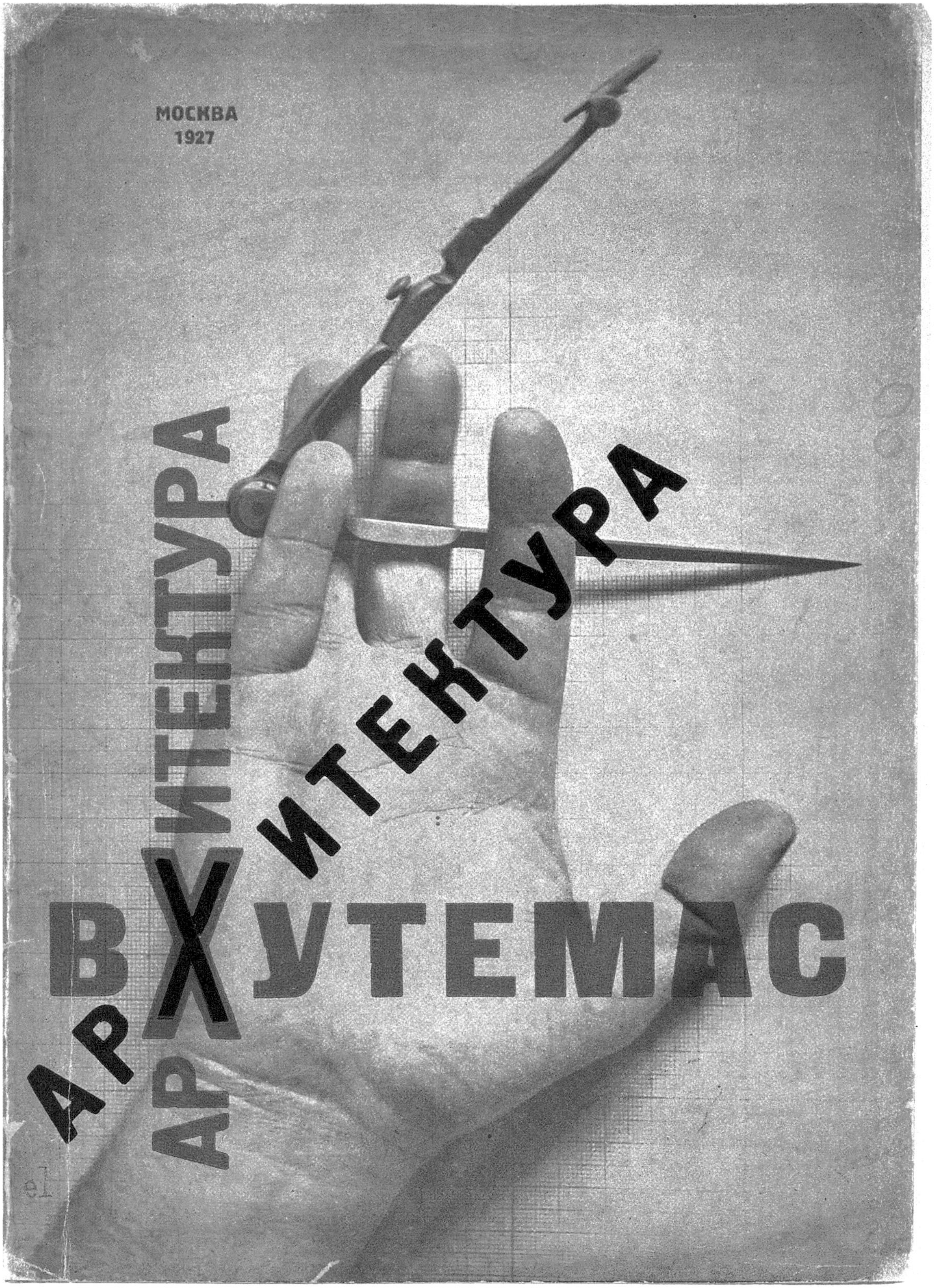
МОСКВА
1927
АРХИТЕКТУРА
АРХИТЕКТУРА
ВХУТЕМАС
el

Plate 14

*All-Union Printing Trades
Exhibition. Catalogue*, 1927,
cover by El Lissitzky
(Cup.410.e.87).

showing, but official criticism barred further productions until Meyerhold produced it again in a revised version for May Day in 1921; afterwards it was shown throughout the Soviet Union. By then Mayakovsky had revised the text to accommodate political changes in the intervening years and, despite continuing criticism, the new text was printed twice in 1922.[25]

It is a measure of the success of the avant-garde that after 1917 artists and writers were involved mainly in productions by the professional directors who dominated the theatre world, rather than being obliged to mount their own plays. An isolated, but significant, exception was the staging of Khlebnikov's poem, *Zangezi*, at the Petrograd Museum of Artistic Culture in May 1923 by Tatlin, who designed and directed the amateur production. Khlebnikov had finished his text in January 1922 and it had been published later the same year with a printed cover bearing a drawing by his brother-in-law, Petr Miturich.[26] In his preface the poet likened his 'supertale' to 'a sculpture made from a chunk of vari-coloured ores, the body – of white stone, the clothes and cloak – of blue stone, the eyes – of black stone ...'.[27] For his printed book cover [65] Miturich did not attempt to draw such a sculpture, with its connotations of a human body; instead, he made a drawing related to ones on his 'spatial graphics' – complex handmade three-dimensional paper sculptures, a little like pop-up books, composed from box-like forms, which he decorated with black and white designs. One of them was a project for poems by Khlebnikov which would have provided a most unusual format for a book; another is covered with drawings of tree-like shapes,[28] which the artist modified for his *Zangezi* cover design, using branching forms ending in leaf-like curlicues and free-flowing loops to suggest both forms from nature and abstracted writing. Miturich developed them from patterns on his better-known 'Graphic dictionary' of 1919, which consists of hundreds of handmade decorated paper cubes which he made as illustrations of Khlebnikov's astral alphabet.[29]

Miturich worked at the Petrograd Museum of Artistic Culture, as did Tatlin, who planned the staging of *Zangezi* at the museum by making a model and drawings of the set. He already had considerable experience of theatre design because, as well as designs for folk plays in 1913, he had made designs for *The Flying Dutchman* in 1917.[30] His set for *Zangezi* – published as a sketch and model in two photographs [66] in the first number of the journal *Russian Art (Russkoe iskusstvo)*[31] – took the form of a three-dimensional structure, more closely related to his projected tower for the Monument to the Third International (76) than his previous work in the theatre. Like Miturich, Tatlin ignored Khlebnikov's description of a sculpture, though he paid lip-service to the steep rock covered by pines from which Zangezi read his sermons, by placing the hero high up above the stage. He wanted his staging to convey the variety of Khlebnikov's complex subject which was described by Iury Tynianov as:

> *a romantic drama (in the sense in which Novalis used this word), where mathematical computations become a new poetic material, where numbers and letters are linked with the downfall of cities and kingdoms, the life of a new poet with the singing of birds, and laughter and grief are necessary for serious irony ...*[32]

For the two characters, Grief and Laughter, Tatlin made elaborate costumes, but he used coloured boards to represent letters of the alphabet – 'V' was green, 'B' red, 'S' grey and so on. To give them a semblance of life he shone searchlights on the boards which were raised and lowered as he directed.

66
Russian Art, No.1, 1923,
p.20: photographs of
drawing and model of set
by V.Tatlin for his
production of *Zangezi*
(PP.1931.pmh).

67
A.Globa, *Tamar. A Tragedy*,
1923, woodcut cover by
V.Favorsky (X.900/20598).

     In complete contrast to Miturich's cover design for *Zangezi* is one for
Andrei Globa's tragedy, *Tamar (Famar'. Tragediia)*[33] made by the distinguished
graphic designer, Vladimir Favorsky, who was appointed Professor in the Faculty
of Graphic Art at *VKhUTEMAS* in 1922 (he was the Rector of the Studios from 1923 to
1925). Favorsky is better known in Russia than in the West,[34] but, as can be seen in
his cover [67] and illustrations for *Tamar*, he was a master of wood engraving.
Although this may seem an unexpected medium for a modern artist, and

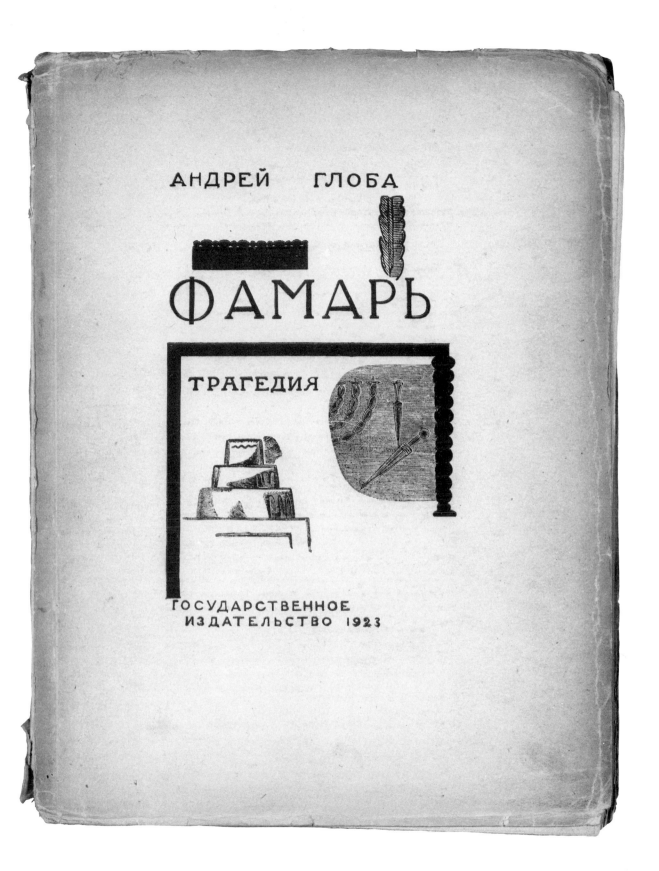

АНДРЕЙ ГЛОБА

ФАМАРЬ

ТРАГЕДИЯ

ГОСУДАРСТВЕННОЕ
ИЗДАТЕЛЬСТВО 1923

Favorsky had no fear of figurative art, he arranged his motifs in a wholly unexpected way, borrowing spatial devices from abstract art. His illustrations for *Tamar* convey the action in a vivid way calling to mind 'agit' posters and cinema. His contiguous arrangement of figures and scenes is related to the cartoon-like arrangement on some *ROSTA* posters; each scene is joined psychologically by the action it portrays but separated by different spatial devices which suggest the frames of a film. Favorsky's work must be judged without reference to the graphic work of his contemporaries because his style can only be described as archaic. This was recognized as early as 1923 in an article published in *Russian Art* No.1, by Abram Efros, who pointed to Favorsky's debt to Dürer, because he allowed the specific quality of wood engraving its full rein and did not use it to imitate other techniques as many recent exponents had done.[35]

 Tamar has to be considered simply as a book design, as does Olga Forsh's *Rabbi (Ravvi)*. Forsh wrote the play under the pseudonym 'A. Terek' and the edition illustrated here [68] was 'included in the repertoire of the Petrograd Studio of the Itinerants Theatre' (*vkliuchena v repertuar "Masterskoi peredvizhnogo teatra" v Peterburge*) though it was published in Berlin with a cover by Lissitzky.[36] *Rabbi* was announced as a new publication in the journal *Object*[37] in April, so Lissitzky's cover for the play belongs among the first that he designed in Berlin; it bears no relation to the subject of the play and belongs in the sequence of inventive designs he made in Berlin, discussed in Chapter 3. There Lissitzky's book cover designs were compared with those by Rodchenko; among theatre books there is also a possible connection: between Rodchenko's cover for Mayakovsky's play *The Bed Bug (Klop)* of 1929[38] and Lissitzky's for the catalogue of the All-Union Exhibition of Printing[39] of two years before. *The Bed Bug* has a particularly unusual cover design [plate 13]; it is unsigned but attributed to Rodchenko,[40] who left the four capital letters '*KLOP*' the colour of the cover, making them readable by overprinting bands of solid blue and speckled brown which give the illusion of being 'behind' the letters. Lissitzky had used rather similar speckled colouring, in silver on red, for his exhibition catalogue [plate 14]. It is not unlikely that Rodchenko was inspired in his choice of an unusual technique by what he had seen at this comprehensive display of printing techniques and equipment.

 As well as designing the book cover, Rodchenko had been involved in stage design for *The Bed Bug*. The director was Meyerhold, who remained appreciative of Mayakovsky as a dramatist and produced both *The Bed Bug* and a second satirical drama, *The Bath House (Bania)*[41] in 1929 and 1930. In both, Mayakovsky criticized what he saw as the betrayal of revolutionary ideals begun with Lenin's New Economic Policy, which, he felt, had promoted the continuance of bourgeois values. Even though the productions were disliked by officialdom, they were popular with audiences – of all Soviet plays which Meyerhold produced *The Bed Bug* has been revived most often.[42] The plot, which is based on a filmscript written by Mayakovsky in 1927,[43] required two styles of design. The first, for scenes set in the present, was carried out by the young cartoonists, the Kukryniksy,[44] who chose most of the costumes and props from what was on sale in Moscow shops. The second, for an imaginary future world, was carried out by Rodchenko in what today would be called a 'science fiction' manner. The hero, a lapsed party-member named Prisypkin, disappeared in a fire which broke out during his drunken wedding orgy; his corpse was frozen and brought back to life by a future generation living 'ten Five Year Plans' hence. Mayakovsky contrasted

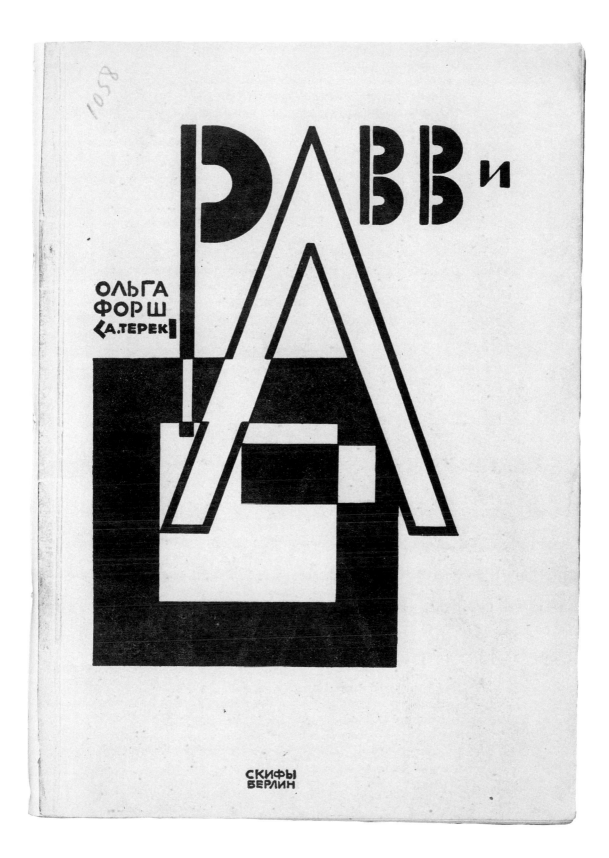

РАВВи

ОЛЬГА
ФОРШ
А.ТЕРЕК

СКИФЫ
БЕРЛИН

117

the vulgar Prisypkin with the hygienic, clinical workers of the future; in their world the only suitable place for Prisypkin was a cage in a zoo where he could be observed like an animal. The final ironic moment was when the caged hero invited the audience – which Mayakovsky saw as neo-bourgeois like Prisypkin – to take their places on the stage beside him. The title of the play was provided by Prisypkin's companion, the bed bug which had been frozen and survived the thaw with him. Rodchenko's typographic cover design suggests neither his own Constructivist set and costumes, nor the Kukryniksy's contemporary Moscow, but this is, of course, a normal feature of published plays. The typographic cover for Mayakovsky's *The Bath House* – made by A. Surikov [69] – was less interesting, though it is a respectable Constructivist design, following the examples of Rodchenko and Lissitzky.

Mayakovsky was not the only writer to attempt plays for a new public. His colleague Tretiakov, who was responsible for the text of *The Earth Rampant* discussed above, wrote the play *Can You Hear, Moscow?! (Slyshish', Moskva?!)*[45] which he described as an 'agit-guignol' – roughly speaking, a propagandized Punch and Judy show. The text was unashamedly political, a response to political revolution in Germany, so the cast was made up of German Communist workers and their antagonists, the police, a bishop and a representative of American banks. No doubt the intention was to encourage Russian workers to feel part of an international revolutionary movement because, on the page opposite the list of characters, the reader is informed that the play was to be produced on 16 October 1924 by Proletkult Workers' Clubs simultaneously in eleven cities – among them Moscow, Petrograd, Tula, Saratov and Tiflis. Five thousand copies of the text were printed in 1923, well in advance, though a delay resulted in a 1924 publication date on the cover of the slim but large booklet. There is no indication of the name of the designer of its simple black lettering and pairs of thick green lines separating text at top and bottom [70]. At the time Tretiakov headed the First Workers' Theatre of the Proletkult with Sergei Eisenstein, and the cover indicates that the play was one in a series of 'Proletarian repertoire'. Eisenstein had produced the play in 1923 but his addition of circus turns – with acrobats diving from high up and trapeze artistes flying through the air and walking tightropes – must have diminished Tretiakov's dialogue. Eisenstein went so far as to have one of the characters, a courtesan, make her stage entrance riding a camel, which was totally irrelevant to the play and difficult for local Proletkult groups to emulate![46]

Proletkult theatres continued to operate throughout the 1920s and a later example of the publication of a play in the repertoire is the striking cover [71] for a small edition of Aleksandr Afinogenov's drama, *At the Turning Point (Na perelome, (v riady))*;[47] it bears the initials 'K.Z' which have been identified as those of Kirill Zdanevich.[48] The artist – whose earlier work was mentioned in Chapter 2 – divided his time between Tiflis and Moscow in the 1920s and was in contact with Mayakovsky, for whom he illustrated a children's book, and Kruchenykh, for whom he drew a cover design (*see* 17).[49] *At the Turning Point* is unlike Zdanevich's other work: the letters are superimposed on a fusion of typographic elements; these are not, however, entirely abstract because the black rectangles can be read as blank windows. The cover is more distinguished than the play itself: Afinogenov's early plays are of interest mainly for their record of contemporary Soviet life; popular success eluded him until 1931.[50]

60 к.

В. МАЯКОВСКИЙ

баня

ГОСУДАРСТВЕННОЕ ИЗДАТЕЛЬСТВО 1930

119

РЕПЕРТУАР ПРОЛЕТКУЛЬТА.

С. Третьяков.

СЛЫШИШЬ, МОСКВА?!

Агит-гиньоль в 4-х действиях.

ВСЕРОССИЙСКИЙ ПРОЛЕТКУЛЬТ.

Москва—1924.

Tretiakov achieved greater success with his plays. His *Roar, China!
(Rychi Kitai!)* – was published in the journal *LEF* in 1924[51] and produced in
Meyerhold's theatre during that season.[52] Meyerhold then spent several years
trying to find the right way to stage Tretiakov's controversial *I Want a Child
(Khochu rebenka)*. This thought-provoking play addresses the problem of the role
of the family in the new society (discussed in the Introduction). Tretiakov chose a
Communist rural economist for his heroine; she wants neither the ties of a
family, nor unlimited 'free love', so she chooses a healthy father to give her a baby
and relieve her sexual tensions.[53] The play was accepted by Meyerhold in 1926
and the text was printed in *New LEF* the following year.[54] The censor, however,
found the plot unsuitable for the stage and Meyerhold spent four years trying to
overcome the opposition. He envisaged staging it with the audience participating
in the discussion of the contentious but topical issue, and Lissitzky designed a
special setting in the round.[55] Construction of the set had to be postponed until
Meyerhold achieved a new theatre building, but the project was never realized. In
December 1937, the play, which had been a truthful attempt to address a complex
social problem, was described as a 'hostile slur on the Soviet family' by the
'enemy of the people, Tretiakov' in the article 'An Alien Theatre' published in
Pravda.[56] By that time the family unit was no longer considered a bourgeois
survival but valued as a contribution to the stability of society.

During the 1930s Meyerhold found it increasingly difficult to work in
the climate of Socialist Realism, especially as he was loath to compromise his
progressive ideas. The book of essays which takes its title from his production of
Tchaikovsky's opera, *Queen of Spades (Pikovaia dama)*,[57] at the Maly Theatre bears
witness to the suppression of avant-garde design for books and the stage that had
taken place by 1935. Both staging and book [72] represent a throwback to the more
realistic style which Meyerhold had used in the Imperial theatres before 1917,
though his alteration of the libretto, making it closer to the original poem by
Pushkin, was regarded by some critics as an improvement.[58] The style of the
decor was nearer to Stanislavsky's naturalistic approach than to Meyerhold's
own post-Revolutionary Constructivist productions; the book itself, with its cover
by L. T. Chupiatov and tipped-in plates, seems like a throw-back to one designed by
Sergei Chekhonin in 1923 to record the Moscow Arts Theatre production of the
nineteenth-century play, *Woe from Wit (Gore ot uma)*.[59] Meyerhold produced that
classic himself in 1935 in his attempt to continue working in an unfavourable
climate. He was, however, unable to remain silent; a conference speech shortly
after the death of Stanislavsky led to his immediate arrest[60] and brought this era
of theatrical innovation to an end.

Even from this brief survey of books devoted to Soviet theatre it is
clear that major artists were attracted to the stage, as designers of scenery and
costumes and as designers of publications recording theatre. Compared to
designing the cover for a book of poetry or a novel, theatre design proved
fascinating to artists because, like architecture, it provided the opportunity to use
a third dimension. Unlike architecture, however, the artist generally shared his
vision with that of a director for whom he was often visualizing ideas. This was a
stimulating way to work and it is clear that many of these theatre publications
reflect the enthusiasm generated by the productions.

5

Utopian Ideas in Art and Architecture

The books and journals on art and architecture reproduced here provide a record of Utopian ideas in post-Revolutionary Russia. The fundamental difference, however, between the heroes of the theatre world discussed in Chapter 4 and the architects who form the principal subject of this chapter lies in their pre-1917 activities. Progressive ideas in Russian theatre had been continuous from the beginning of the twentieth century and the events of 1917 simply accelerated experiments already far developed; in contrast, Russian architecture had seen no such advances. By 1917 no architect had the stature of Tairov and Meyerhold: in the field of architecture Russia was not a world leader, though it was to become so by the end of the 1920s. The reason for the delay was that Art Nouveau buildings had convinced most Russian architects that Neo-Classicism was preferable to what they termed the 'Modern Style' and most inventive structures had been the work of engineers rather than architects.[1]

After the Bolsheviks took power, Lunacharsky supported the prevailing neo-classical bias of Russian architecture and in 1920 explained that he had split off the sub-section for architecture from *IZO* – the Fine Art Section of *Narkompros* – 'where a keen mood of experimentation and Leftist art tendencies prevailed' – because:

… architecture does not tolerate such bold ventures. It is our first priority, in so far as architecture is concerned, to find a firm base in classical traditions correctly understood. I thought it essential that the People's Commissariat should have its own qualified architectural art staff capable of laying the foundations of a great Communist construction drive, by the time this becomes a practical possibility, and to give it aesthetic direction.[2]

None the less there were a few forward-looking architects in *Izo* and they formed a Commission for the Synthesis of Painting, Sculpture and Architecture (*Zhivskulptarkh*) in 1919, independent of the classicist Artistic Section of Architecture. Many of the most original ideas subsequently explored came from painters, especially from Rodchenko, who was invited to join the group on its inauguration at the end of the year. The Soviet architectural historian, Selim Khan-Magomedov, believes that Rodchenko was able to contribute ways of exploring formal problems that enabled architects radically to rethink the manner in which they had been trained, just because he had no formal architectural training himself.[3] Moreover, Futurist artists in particular were more aware of and sympathetic to the idea of restructuring life, which became a priority after the Revolution. These artists were more open to the admonitions of an Italian Futurist 'Manifesto of Architecture' in which Antonio Sant'Elia had insisted: 'It is a question of ... determining new forms, new lines, a new harmony of profiles and volumes, an architecture whose reason for existence can be found solely in the unique conditions of modern life' ... 'modern constructional materials and scientific concepts are absolutely incompatible with the disciplines of historical style' ... 'we have enriched our sensibility with a taste for the light, the practical, the ephemeral and the swift'.[4]

Whether or not this 1914 manifesto paved a way, the Revolution provided the incentive for finding new architectural forms in which to embody a new social system. The role of the family was one of the most seriously discussed issues in the 1920s; the family household versus communal housing was an issue which directly concerned architects and provided much discussion later in the decade in architectural journals. Already in 1920 experimental designs for a housing commune were produced by Nikolai Ladovsky and others in *Zhivskulptarkh*;[5] members of the group were to prove some of the most progressive individuals in the visual arts.

Turning from architects to painters and sculptors, Russians were at the forefront of the European avant-garde by the second decade of the century, though their inventions were often less well-known abroad than those of theatre designers. There were exceptions: paintings and drawings by Marc Chagall were better known in Europe than in his home country because he had lived in Paris between 1910 and 1914 and shown his work at the gallery Der Sturm in Berlin. A short visit to his home in Vitebsk in the summer of 1914 was prolonged because of the outbreak of war and, in the following years in Russia, he attempted to find a new form for Jewish art. This enjoyed a brief flowering in 1917-18, after years of systematic suppression of Jewish culture, and was especially fruitful in the field of book illustration.[6] In summer 1918, Chagall set up an Art School and Museum in his home-town under the auspices of *Narkompros*. The same year saw the publication of *The Art of Marc Chagall (Iskusstvo Marka Shagala)*,[7] a substantial monograph by the critics Abram Efros and Iakov Tugendkhold, with a cover design by the artist [73]. It included photographs of many of Chagall's early works which he had left in Western Europe in 1914. But his street decorations in Vitebsk for the anniversary of the Revolution were disliked: his flying cows proved as utopian and unacceptable as any of the abstract art put up in Moscow or Petrograd on the same occasion. Chagall's position as Commissar for the Arts and Theatre in Vitebsk became untenable after Lissitzky and Malevich joined the Art School staff in 1919 and began using the facilities of the Graphics Department to produce books extolling Suprematism as the correct method for modern art.[8] Malevich's position seemed assured when the main thrust of his argument from *On New Systems in Art (O novykh sistemakh v iskusstve)*[9] was reissued the following year by *Narkompros* as an 'official' account of modernist art, under the title *From Cézanne to Suprematism (Ot Sezanna do suprematizma. Kriticheskii ocherk)*.[10] Whereas *On New Systems in Art* was hand-produced in the Art School by transfer lithography, with a linocut cover by Lissitzky, the abbreviated version was conventionally printed with an undistinguished typographic cover bearing only the title and author's name. This casts the pamphlet in the role of a text-book

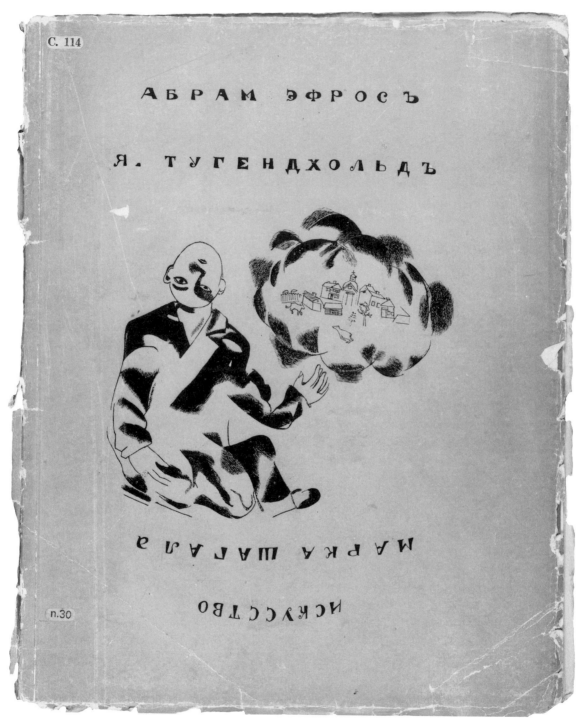

АБРАМ ЭФРОСЪ

Я. ТУГЕНДХОЛЬДЪ

МАРКА ШАГАЛА

ИСКУССТВО

73
A. Efros and Ia.
Tugendkhold, *The Art of
Marc Chagall*, 1918, cover
by M. Chagall (C.114.n.30).

74 ▷
Artist's Text, 1918, cover by
V. Kandinsky (C.104.i.16).

КАНДИНСКİЙ

introduction to twentieth-century art, but Malevich was not the type of artist to fulfil a simplistic pedagogic role; with Lissitzky he formed a new association at the Art School – *UNOVIS* – an acronym standing for 'Affirmation of the New Art'.[11] Their aim was to use Suprematist art not simply for easel painting but for street decorations, posters, book covers[12] and even porcelain and architecture. Members of *UNOVIS* included Klutsis and Senkin, who became Constructivist designers and made photomontages discussed in Chapter 3. Other members remained loyal to Malevich: Lazar Khidekel, Nikolai Suetin and Ilia Chashnik distinguished themselves as architects after *UNOVIS* moved to Petrograd in 1922.

Two more theoretical texts by Malevich were published before he left Vitebsk: the first, *On the Question of Fine Art (K voprosu izobrazitel'nogo iskusstva)*,[13] was issued by the State Publishing House in Smolensk in 1921 with an unaccountably amateurish cover design of a square within a square; the second, a forty-four page pamphlet with an uninteresting printed cover entitled, *God is not Cast Down. Art, Church, Factory (Bog ne skinut. Iskusstvo. Tserkov'. Fabrika)* was published in Vitebsk.[14] Neither was illustrated and the best records of Malevich's painting remain the slim, hand-produced, *Suprematism. 34 Drawings (Suprematizm. 34 risunki)*[15] that lacked the colour so central to his work, and the printed book cover for Punin's *First Cycle of Lectures (Pervyi tsikl lektsii)* bearing an example of Malevich's Suprematist forms in colour [plate 15].[16] Inspired by Suprematism, Lissitzky evolved his *Prouns* – easel paintings with names such as 'Town' and 'Bridge' – which he described as a junction between painting and architecture; they provided the basis for his subsequent work in the field of architecture, where he became active in publishing his own ideas and those of his colleagues in the Soviet Union and Western Europe in numerous journals and books, considered later in this chapter. Book illustration by Chagall, who left Vitebsk first for Moscow and then for Berlin and Paris, falls outside the scope of this study, though he contributed greatly to book art in France in the 1920s and 1930s through the patronage of Ambroise Vollard.[17]

Vasily Kandinsky, like Chagall, had made his reputation in Western Europe and did not return to live in Russia until 1916. He was considerably older than other avant-garde artists and was given a good deal of responsibility in *IZO*; *Narkompros* soon published his *Artist's Text (V.V.Kandinskii. Tekst khudozhnika)*.[18] Although this was not an up-to-date statement of his principles – being a Russian translation of his 1913 'Reminiscences'[19] – the photographs of recent paintings reproduced in the book and the drawing on the cover [74] affirmed his radical approach which was confirmed by his contribution to the journal *Fine Art* on the topic of stage composition. Kandinsky proclaimed 'a new world which combines individual art forms within a single work' – 'the world of Monumental Art';[20] his other texts printed at the time include articles 'On Point' and 'On Line'.[21] For a time Rodchenko lived in Kandinsky's Moscow apartment[22] so it is not surprising that he took the opportunity to develop his own painting into three dimensions by joining *Zhivskulptarkh*; no doubt the older artist's researches inspired Rodchenko's rival text 'On Line'.[23] Both artists were involved during the following year in the setting up of the Moscow Institute of Artistic Culture (*INKhUK*) as a laboratory for the scientific investigation of art. Kandinsky chaired the Praesidium and his notion of monumental art as a '*Gesamtkunstwerk*', uniting painting, music, dance and poetry, was explored for the first months together with the psychology of perception. He devised a plan for a psycho-physiological

ЦИКЛ

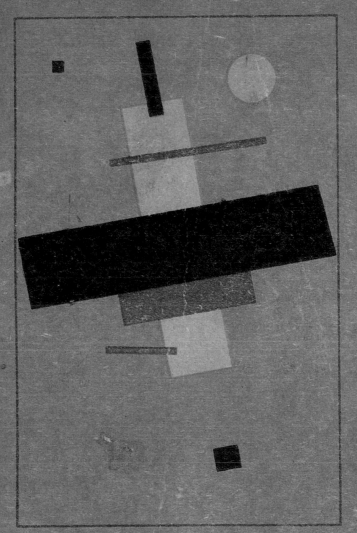

ЛЕКЦИЙ
н.н. ПУНИНА.

Всесоюзная

Полиграфическая

Выставка

ПУТЕВОДИТЕЛЬ

МОСКВА

1927

laboratory at the Institute,[24] but his programme, which included investigation into the spiritual and occult dimensions of art, was soon opposed by younger artists, including Rodchenko, who believed that the future of painting lay in sculpture and architecture, and their creation of a new environment. The disagreements were exacerbated by differing approaches to applied psychology: the Institute became increasingly involved in industrial design and contemporary notions of scientific management – best subsumed under the writings of Frederick Taylor discussed earlier in this study – whereas Kandinsky's ideas seem closer to the type of experimental psychology practised at the time in the United States and Germany, and popularized in the writings of Hugo Münsterburg, who described experiments in his own laboratory and in many areas of psychological research.[25] Although the architect Ladovsky joined Rodchenko's Working Group for Objective Analysis formed at *INKhUK* in opposition to Kandinsky, later on, with a breakaway group of like-minded colleagues (who called themselves Rationalists), Ladovsky set up his own psychotechnical laboratory which was run on the lines of Münsterburg's research. Experiments were undertaken to discover the aptitude of new students for architecture, as well as to test spatial combinations and to 'verify the impact of architectural elements on the human psyche'.[26] So, although Kandinsky resigned from *INKhUK* and left Russia for Germany, programmes related to his own were continued by Ladovsky and his Rationalist group.

Kandinsky resigned during three months of debate at the Institute on the 'Analysis of the concepts of construction and composition and the dividing line between them'. A record of these discussions was not published at the time, but the disagreements resulted in the formation of groupings which had far-reaching consequences for art and architecture in Russia and beyond. The primary division occurred between Ladovsky's Rationalists and Rodchenko's Constructivist supporters, who set up the first Working Group of Constructivists in spring 1921. By April, Gan had drawn up their programme which included the decision to pass from laboratory work to real activity and practical experiments; Constructivists believed that new art should help to create a new environment. Gan's ideas on Constructivism were embodied in his book of the same title published the following year. The architectural historian, Catherine Cooke, has pointed out that available translations give a false impression of the book by omitting Gan's long quotations from the Communist Manifesto and his advocacy of architecture and the urban environment as material for Constructivists: the 'primary objective' of their 'definite system', Gan maintained, must be 'to establish a scientific foundation for the approach to constructing buildings and services that would fulfil the demands of Communist culture in its transient state, through all stages of its future development out of this period of ruin.'[27]

Before Gan's book was published, a further split took place, when Brik joined *INKhUK* in the autumn of 1921 and identified current thinking there as Constructivism and 'Veshchizm' – literally, the 'culture of things'; he criticized artists of both trends for not progressing to Productivism. Brik was among the contributors to the book, *Production Art (Iskusstvo v proizvodstve* No.1),[28] where the theory of Productivism was set out. The modest hand-drawn look of the cover by Shterenberg [75] belies the ferocity of Brik's argument: 'We know that so-called pure art is the same craft as any other. We do not understand why a man who makes pictures is spiritually superior to one who manufactures fabrics'.[29] While opposing Constructivism and its extreme form, Productivism, Rationalist architects at first agreed with *'Veshchism'*. The term no doubt gave the title to the journal *Object (Veshch'/Gegandstand/Objet)* which Lissitzky and Erenburg founded in 1922 in Berlin; its comprehensive platform, however, blurred distinctions which were more precise within the Soviet Union, for Erenburg wrote: 'Everything, a house, a poem or a picture, structured on constructive principles, helps people to organize life.'[30]

The contents as well as Lissitzky's layout of the two numbers of *Object* (the first was a double number) show a remarkable conjunction of avant-garde ideas from many different sources. For example, in *Object* No.3, Malevich's *Black Square* – the *tabula rasa* of non-objective painting – is reproduced next to a photograph of a locomotive – a favourite motif of Productivists;[31] the same number includes an article on French Purism. Lissitzky was evidently far more catholic than those he had left behind in Moscow and was unaware of the intensity of the disagreements which had split factions there. This allowed him on the one hand to publish work by Rationalist architects in the journal *ABC* and, on the other, to attend international Constructivist conferences and name himself a 'book constructor' on the title-page of Mayakovsky's *For the Voice*.[32]

Constructivism is often discussed as a 'style' – especially in the field of book design – but the original protagonists saw it not as the way things might be made to look different but as a means for shaping the new society. This is even true of the proto-Constructivist Monument to the Third International designed by Tatlin in 1919. Although best known in the version shown on the cover [76] of a book by Punin (*Pamiatnik III Internatsionala*) the monument was not always conceived in spiral form. Describing it in *Art of the Commune* in March 1919, Punin wrote: 'A succession of the simplest forms (cubes) is to contain halls for lectures and gymnastics, premises for agitation and other rooms'. The building was to have 'wings', one of the spaces being a garage, so that 'special motorcycles and cars could constitute a highly mobile, continuously available tool of agitation for the government.'[33] This sounds a more prosaic concept than the final project, more closely related to architecture than sculpture, to utilitarian purpose than the image of modernity. The revised design for a Utopian tower called forth such eulogies as Viktor Shklovsky's: '… The monument is made of iron, glass and revolution',[34] and soon became the best known image of contemporary Russian art. It is now generally received as the immediate forerunner of Constructivist art, but at the time it could not provide a useful prototype for the development of a modern architecture – whether Constructivist or Rationalist – because the technology to build it had not been invented. The basis of Constructivist architecture resides more certainly in two books written by Moisei Ginzburg: *Rhythm in Architecture (Ritm v arkhitekture)*[35] and *Style and Epoch (Stil' i epokha)*.[36]

Ginzburg was already a trained architect and thoroughly at home in Western Europe, having graduated as an architect from the Milan Accademia degli Belli Arti in 1914. The preface to *Rhythm and Architecture* is dated January 1922; the conventionally printed text provides a comprehensive history of architectural forms from stone henges to baroque churches, illustrated by small black and white drawings by the author, as well as excellent photographs of buildings; text and illustrations show the range of his knowledge. Ginzburg's second book is concerned with contemporary architecture and the text is occasionally reinforced with diagrams. He gave the material in lecture form in

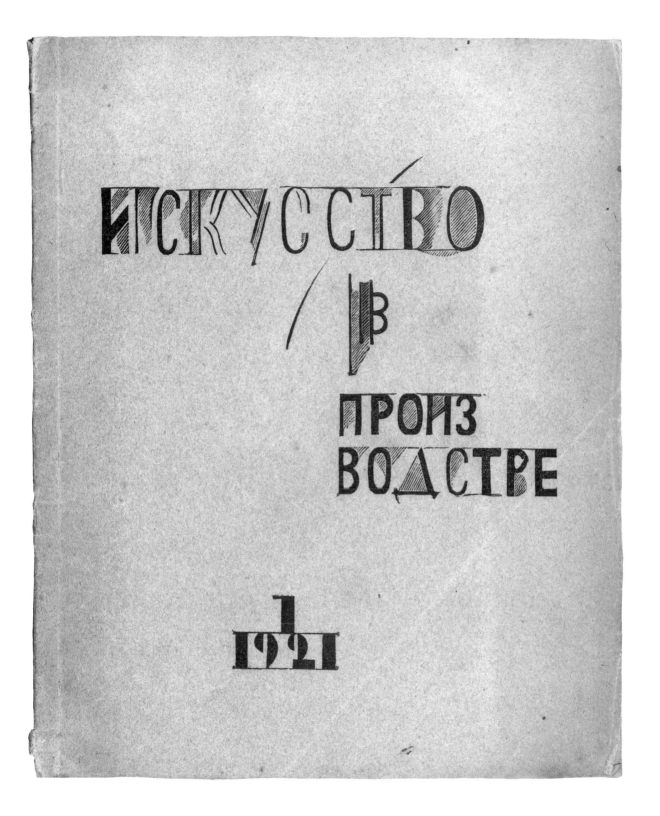

ИСКУССТВО В ПРОИЗ ВОДСТВЕ

1
1921

1923 and the plates provide a record of advanced architectural design up to the
publication date (after February 1924). With the exception of Aleksandr Vesnin's
three-dimensional stage set built for Tairov's production of *The Man Who was
Thursday* [*see* 64] all the designs were projects for the future. They contrast with
the documentary material: photographs of real aeroplanes, grain silos and other
representatives of contemporary design are placed on the opposite page and as
headings to the beginning of chapters.[37] Ginzburg sees them as models for the
present machine age and they are to serve as blueprints for designers and
architects. Whereas the pages of the journal *LEF* trumpeted the admonitions of
Constructivists, Ginzburg couched his arguments in a more persuasive vein.
A phrase from *Style and Epoch* sums up the rationale of Constructivist design:

> *As in other realms of human activity, the machine above all impels us toward
> utmost organization in creative work and toward clarity and precision in formulating a
> creative idea.*[38]

A fuller record of Constructivist building achievements begins in 1926
with the publication of the journal *Contemporary Architecture (Sovremennaia
arkhitektura*, usually abbreviated to *SA).*[39] This was the organ of the Union of
Contemporary Architects – *OSA* – which Constructivist architects had founded at
the close of 1925. The editors were Aleksandr Vesnin and Ginzburg and for the
first year or two the covers and typographic layout were designed by Gan [77]. The
journal was most successful in publicizing contemporary architecture and the
point of view of *OSA* over a long period; the bi-monthly ran continuously from 1926
to 1933 with a change of designers in 1929, when Stepanova and then Telingater
took over from Gan.[40] In contrast, the members of *ASNOVA* produced just one slim
publication, in 1926, a review of their Association of New Architects (*ASNOVA.
Izvestiia Assotsiatsii novykh arkhitektorov).*[41] Its elaborate typographic design is one
of Lissitzky's most mannered productions: on the cover he repeated each of the
five letters, '*A*', '*S*', '*N*', '*O*', '*V*', '*A*' in cyrillic and roman capitals, varying the position
of the letters and reducing the roman letters to one quarter the size of the cyrillic
ones. The design is linked in the minds of Westerners to Constructivism although
it was the organ of the rival Rationalist group, and may, even, look a little Dadaist.
But Lissitzky's slogan, 'Architecture is the measure of architecture', printed on
the bottom of the final page, could be interpreted as a riposte by Rationalists to
insistence by the *OSA* Constructivists that function determines form.

The differences between the two professional organizations – *OSA*, the
Union of Contemporary Architects and *ASNOVA*, the Association of New Architects
– seem at first glance quite subtle. Both insisted on the patriotic nature of their
work: thus, from the *ASNOVA News*, 'The USSR is the builder of a new way of life …
The USSR represents rationalized labour in unity with science and highly
developed technology' and from *SA*, 'There is no other field of artistic labour in
which the events of October produced as decisive, as categorical a revolutionary
change as in architecture.'[42] But reading further, the working methods of
members of the two groups prove to have sprung from rather different premises.
The differing points of view resulted in the schemes and buildings published in
the pages of *SA* – where space was sometimes found for rival *ASNOVA* opinions
and designs – and also in a yearbook for 1927, *Architecture. Works from the
Architecture Faculty at VKhUTEMAS (Arkhitektura. Raboty Arkhitekturnogo fakul'teta
Vkhutemasa).*[43] Photographs chosen for that yearbook have a slight bias towards

Н. ПУНИН

ПАМЯТНИК

III

ИНТЕРНАЦИОНАЛА

Проект худ. В. Е. ТАТЛИНА

ПЕТЕРБУРГ

Издание Отдела Изобразительных Искусств Н. К. П.

1920 г.

133

77

Contemporary Architecture,
No.2, 1926, cover by A. Gan
(C.185.bb.2).

designs by Ladovsky's Rationalist students, and Lissitzky's cover design [plate 16] seems to allude to his own slogan, 'Architecture is the measure of architecture'. None the less, designs by the students of Constructivist teachers were also included. The book was given an unfavourable review in the November number of the middle-of-the-road journal, *The Construction of Moscow (Stroitel'stvo Moskvy),*[44] though six photographs taken from the book were reproduced in this monthly publication.

The same number of the *The Construction of Moscow* included an article on the Workers' Club for the Rusakov factory designed by Konstantin Melnikov, an architect who collaborated with the *ASNOVA* group. The idea of clubs for workers anticipated the Revolution: 'People's Houses' – providing leisure facilities for workers – were set up by the Moscow City Council in an attempt to combat alcoholism in 1915.[45] They were equipped with reading rooms, cinemas, concert platforms and lecture halls and, after the Revolution, Lenin supported the extension of the idea as clubs. As promulgated by the Eighth Party Congress, Workers' Clubs were to be centres for political agitation as well as cultural education for the workers. Some were situated in communal houses and, like them, became the subject of continuous architectural and political debate throughout the decade. In the mid-1920s it appeared that workers were boycotting the clubs and the head of the trade unions proposed that clubs should concentrate on generating 'healthy recreation and healthy laughter' rather than on proselytizing the 'proletarian Revolution and its problems.'[46] There was a great building drive for Workers' Clubs in the later 1920s, trade union leaders gave commissions to the best architects and made sure that the Moscow City Council allowed the plans to go forward. Melnikov – who was commissioned by unions to design at least seven clubs – remembered in later life how plans which he submitted were approved at once and construction began within days! The only problem was money, which often meant that the plans had to be simplified; funds usually ran out before his preferred furnishings could be bought.[47]

Melnikov's Rusakov Workers' Club had an innovative shape, with three auditoria separately cantilevered into space at second-floor level, forming a remarkable façade on the street elevation.[48] The club (which still stands) provides evidence not only of Melnikov's supreme inventiveness but also of the Rationalists' attention to the effect of volumes seen as a whole. The building achieves its aim of providing three auditoria which could be used separately or together as one large space, and they are fused into an adventurous single structure. In contrast, Constructivist architects were so concerned to express the function of each part of a building that they designed them as separate elements and then joined one part to another, often by overhead bridges.[49]

As placed on the cover of *The Construction of Moscow*, Melnikov's drawing of the Rusakov Workers' Club clashes violently with the old-fashioned graphic design of its setting [78]. For several years such oppositions were a standard feature of the journal, typical not only of the cover but of the contents, which included articles on traditional and modern architecture as well as on such subjects as the contents of historical museums. The look of the magazine was updated in January 1928 when it came out with a newly-designed cover by Klutsis and Vasily Elkin, and again the following year, when Telingater took over. His design for the October issue of 1929 [79] still contrasts old with new, but with a definite bias towards contemporary design and architecture. The magazine

СА 2

СОВРЕМЕННАЯ
АРХИТЕКТУРА
ARCHITEKTUR
DER GEGENWART

1926

АЛЕКСЕЙ ГАН.

ГЛАВНОЕ УПРАВЛЕНИЕ НАУЧНЫМИ УЧРЕЖДЕНИЯМИ ■ ГОСУДАРСТВЕННОЕ ИЗДАТЕЛЬСТВО

78
*The Construction of
Moscow*, No.11, 1927, with
K. Melnikov's design for
the Rusakov Workers'
Club inset on a cover
signed 'A.B.R' (PP.8006.uw).

79
*The Construction of
Moscow*, No.10, 1929, cover
by S.Telingater
(PP.8006.uw).

addressed the contemporary problem of suitable furniture for smaller living units, with new, multi-purpose built-in fittings like the one shown on the cover.

In 1925-26 the Moscow City Council organized an All-Union competition for a design for workers' dwellings, specifying 'a type of house suitable both for single workers and working families with no housekeeping facilities of their own'.[50] *SA* also set up an internal competition for the outline design of a new workers' dwelling for the *OSA* exhibition the following year; some proposals were published in the journal. The problem was not simply one of housing but of the expected change in the basic structures of life; in 1923 the feminist writer Aleksandra Kollantai had predicted that:

> ... *the family in its bourgeois sense, will die out. A new force will take its place, the family of the collective of workers in which people will be bound together not by blood relationships but by their common work, their community of interests, aspirations and aims, and which will make them into brothers in spirit.*[51]

The chronic shortage of housing – constantly aggravated by the influx of new workers into cities – meant that as fast as new buildings went up, their planned usage was thwarted by pressure of numbers: communal leisure rooms were appropriated by families and single rooms were used for multi-occupation. Where blocks of three-roomed flats were put up, each room was often taken over by a family, so the communal facilities were grossly oversubscribed. None the less, the concept of communal housing continued to attract architects who sometimes showed an extraordinary degree of insensitivity to their clients. An extreme example is the time-table of a typical worker's day envisaged by Nikolai Kuzmin in an article in *SA* No.3, 1930. He divides the day into twenty-four closely controlled parts, beginning with going to sleep at ten pm so that the worker can have eight hours rest before wake-up time, six am. Five minutes later he has completed his gymnastics and then has ten minutes for washing and another five for an optional shower (Kuzmin does not suggest that the facilities might be too crowded to allow this every day). After five minutes for dressing and three to reach the dining room, the worker is given a quarter of an hour for breakfast, two minutes to reach the cloakroom (where he stores his outdoor clothes) and a further five to reach the pit (this worker is evidently a miner). He stays there until three pm (Kuzmin evidently does not know about shift-work); he has ten minutes to return to the commune and another seven to 'straighten himself out'. A generous eight minutes is allowed for hand-washing before a half-hour meal. The miner is finally allowed recreation in the 'club' where he has a choice of activities including cultural entertainment, athletics, and perhaps swimming; all this is assigned four hours, leaving him just half-an-hour to get to bed.[52] In this Utopia there is no mention of personal relationships – any children are presumably being professionally cared-for in special quarters, and there is no indication of any time when they might receive personal attention from their parents. No wonder, then, that the system was not only unpopular but unworkable, except for single workers just arrived from afar. Indeed *SA* had already warned in an editorial in the first number of 1930:

> ... *the 'false commune' which reduces living space and convenience, with queues for washbasins, lavatories, cloakrooms, canteens, is beginning to arouse anxiety among the working masses. The technical impossibility of creating such rudimentary facilities is evident to the leaders of our economy.*[53]

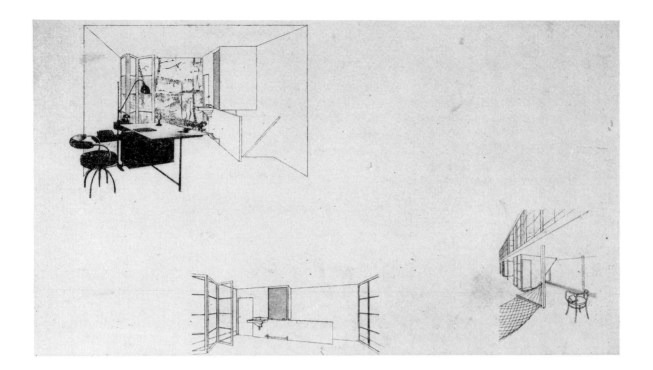

80
Contemporary Architecture,
No.1/2, 1930, p.27: housing
units for Green City
proposal by Barshch and
Ginzburg (C.185.bb.2).

and in an article in the same number, Aleksandr Pasternak added:

> *instead of laundries for twenty-five thousand people and refectories for*
> *thousands, we should have small facilities, that would serve localized areas and be cheaper to*
> *build. In such refectories it will be possible to have dinner in small groups without noise and*
> *crowds.*[54]

In this article Pasternak was discussing the project for a 'Green City' which is illustrated in the same number. The designers, Ginzburg with Mikhail Barshch, appeared to have given up strict functionalism, no doubt because Ginzburg had left his theoretical research in *OSA* in 1928 to head a section of the Committee for Construction of the Russian Republic (*RSFSR*) which was to investigate new types of inexpensive housing. Their plan for a Green City is linear, with housing strung out along roads and public facilities at suitable intervals. They observed only some of the competition rules (published in *The Construction of Moscow* later in 1930) which stipulated plans for a town to accommodate up to a hundred thousand people, with collectivized cooking and transport, to include recreational, cultural and child-care facilities; eleven of the fifteen thousand hectares allotted to the town were to be left as forest.[55] Ginzburg and Barshch imagined terraces of small units of accommodation [80] where couples could have some privacy from one another (though living together):

> *The unit has two façades ... Sunrise and sunset, nature on all sides, all that is*
> *not luxury but the satisfaction of undeniable needs ... The sun traverses the whole of the*
> *housing unit. When the windows are swung back, the unit is transformed into a terrace*
> *surrounded by greenery. The bedroom loses its specific 'bedroom' character almost*
> *completely. It dissolves into nature.*[56]

81
Contemporary Architecture,
No.5, 1930, title-page by
S. Telingater using
I. Leonidov's project for a
Palace of Culture
(C.185.bb.2).

Their proposal – which even showed an elephant roaming the contours of their map[57] – seems almost as far-fetched in the circumstances of Russia's First Five Year Plan as Kuzmin's idea of a typical worker's day outlined above. But the French architectural historian, Anatole Kopp, has pointed out that by the early 1930s Soviet architecture was at the service of a new class of bureaucrats, the managers of the factories, mines and hydraulic power stations which were being built to fulfil the Plan. These managers already had special shops and employed a living-in help to do the housework and look after the children so they did not need communal facilities. He quotes the rationalizations of a chief engineer in some such plant:

> ... I have made a discovery that will bring in a big profit for the State. It is fair and reasonable that I should be able to do my shopping in special shops and that I shall soon have the possibility of enjoying a three-room flat in a new block. As for the Commune, it is a great and noble idea that will certainly exist one day, but at the level of the Russian economy it is utopian, a frenzy for levelling carried to its limits, a leftist deviation of the petit-bourgeois and Trotskyist mind.[58]

Criticisms such as 'leftist deviation' and 'Formalism' were joined by the term 'Leonidovism', coined from extreme designs produced at the end of the 1920s by the Constructivist architect, Leonidov. Telingater composed an unusual title-page for *SA* No.5 of 1930 [81] by using Leonidov's competition design for a 'Palace of Culture' for the Moscow Proletarsky district. The issue was devoted to discussion of Palaces of Culture, which were an extension of the Workers' Club idea on an altogether grander scale – Leonidov's buildings, shown in a park-like setting, include a pyramid, two domes and a horizontal building raised on stilts. They are all strung out in a line with an airship moored overhead. Curiously, the plan does not conform to the elevations, being placed in reverse: this may have been Telingater's oversight or a deliberate design choice.

Competitions aroused so much dispute among architectural factions at the end of the decade that the replacement of groups by a single Union of Soviet Architects by decree in April 1932 seemed to members of the profession surprisingly positive. A new journal, *Architecture of the USSR (Arkhitektura SSSR)*[59] replaced the partisan *SA*, its sober cover designed by El Lissitzky [82]. In its first years of publication, *Architecture of the USSR* included articles by twelve leading Moscow architects who were each made director of their own design studio under the Moscow City Council in 1933. After a year, Melnikov published an optimistic report of his studio's progress under the Utopian title 'On the creative self-feeling of an architect':

> Conditions for peaceful activity and for belief in the results of creative work have been created, instead of the organisational and administrative confusion that frequently prevailed ... No longer are there those fruitless scholastic debates over styles which occupied the lion's share of one's time ...[60]

This article was printed after August 1934 when the All-Union Writers' Congress had taken place.[61] Despite its prescription of Socialist Realism as the preferred style for the arts, buildings require so much longer than other forms of art to take shape that many under construction were built, though later criticized as Formalist. During the autumn a first All-Union Conference of Soviet Architects was held in Moscow to work out an agenda for a Congress planned to follow.[62] At the conference the former Constructivists Ginzburg and Aleksandr Vesnin were

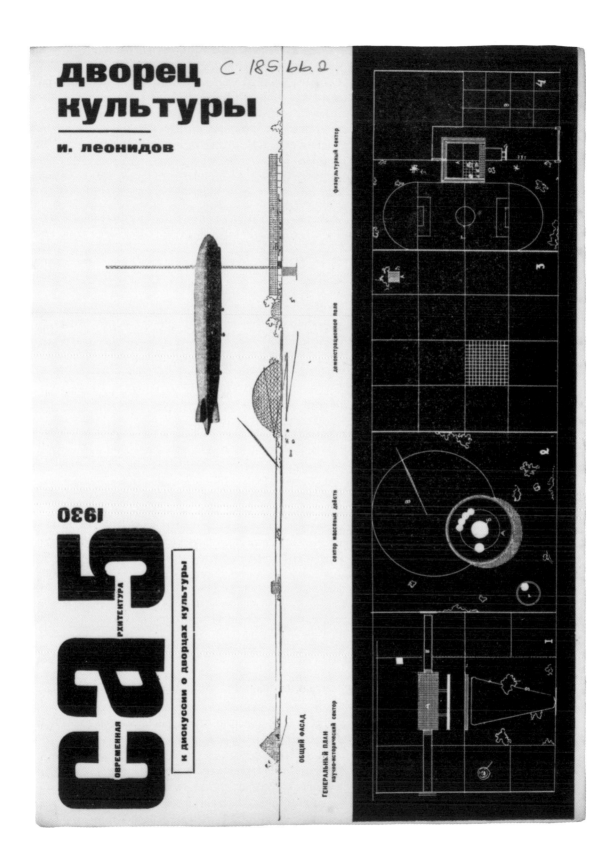

дворец культуры

и. леонидов

СА 5

СОВРЕМЕННАЯ АРХИТЕКТУРА

1930

к дискуссии о дворцах культуры

ОБЩИЙ ФАСАД

ГЕНЕРАЛЬНЫЙ ПЛАН
научно-исторический сектор

сектор массовых действ

демонстрационное поле

физкультурный сектор

141

82
Architecture of the USSR,
No.1, 1934, cover by El
Lissitzky (PP.1667.h).

criticized as nihilists and Melnikov (who had not been invited to attend) was dubbed leader of the Moscow Formalists in his absence.[63] It is significant that the critics were mainly architects from capitals of the outer Republics who no doubt felt that they had been deprived of commissions by Moscow architects.[64]

In discussions on the application of Socialist Realism to architecture, three styles were considered suitable: Neo-Classical, based on the Renaissance; a blend of Oriental and exotic motifs; and New York skyscraper design, which could combine elements from the first two. The third became the preferred option: an exemplar is the grandiose prize-winning design for the Palace of the Soviets by Boris Iofan, which occupied so much space in *Architecture of the USSR* and *The Construction of Moscow* and, as a model, dominated the Soviet Pavilion at the 1937 Paris Universal Exhibition.[65] The great memorial to the decade is, however, the Moscow Metro with its new stations, which were also featured in these architectural journals. Pages of *The Construction of Moscow* record the change from the rather simple, spacious designs of the earliest stations to ones with more and more elaborately decorated walls and ceilings, with rounded arches and soaring spaces resembling a modern version of Piranesi's engravings – which were published in several editions between 1934 and 1938 and reviewed in the journal[66] and served as an unlikely prototype.

In this climate, it is not surprising that the inventive architectural ideas of the architect Chernikhov – which he published in several systematized books – were ignored or thought retrograde. Today they may seem to provide an innocent fund of possible forms for industrial or monumental buildings. But even in 1930 when his first book was published by the Leningrad Society of Architects, Chernikhov was labouring under a disadvantage because he was based in Leningrad. All the architects discussed so far lived and worked in Moscow: Leningrad architects rarely succeeded in getting their buildings published in the pages of *SA*. Chernikhov's first book had the ambitious title, *Fundamentals of Contemporary Architecture. Investigative and Experimental Studies (Osnovy sovremennoi arkhitektury. Eksperimental'no-issledovatel'skie raboty)*[67] but in Moscow, where committees of architects were carrying out detailed scientific studies into maximum living space at minimum cost, his book no doubt seemed irrelevant because it was too generalized. When reviewed in *SA* shortly after publication, it was regarded an anachronism, more relevant in 1921-22 when 'Symbolic' formalism might have been of interest.[68] A second book published by the same author in 1931 'approved by the State council for Academic Affairs' was on ornament. Called *Ornament. Classically Composed Structures (Ornament. Kompozitsionno-klassicheskie postroeniia)*,[69] it was a practical textbook aimed at students, with illustrations of correct and incorrect ways to draw, colour, etc., and it seems remarkable today for its myriad of geometric conceits generated without the help of a computer [83]. However, as most architects at the time favoured plain surfaces or, if they were traditionalists, frankly Neo-Classical ornament, its message can have been of little interest to them. Chernikhov was able to publish two more substantial books of designs in the early 1930s, *The Construction of Architectural and Mechanical Forms (Konstruktsiia arkhitekturnykh i mashinnykh form)*[70] and *Architectural Fantasies (Arkhitekturnye fantazii. 101 kompozitsiia v kraskakh)*.[71] The latter is an amazing compendium of one hundred and one coloured inventions which still excite the imagination today, yet, in the context of architectural projects illustrated in the journals discussed in this chapter, even

СССР

АРХИТЕКТУРА

L'architecture de l'URSS

Architecture of the USSR

Architektur der UdSSR

1
9
3
4

ЖУРНАЛЬНО-ГАЗЕТНОЕ ОБЪЕДИНЕНИЕ

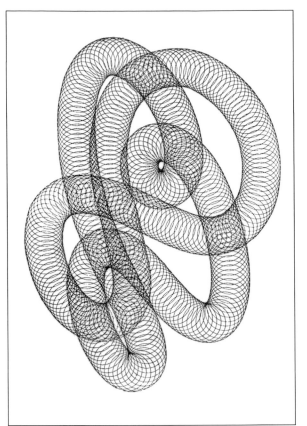

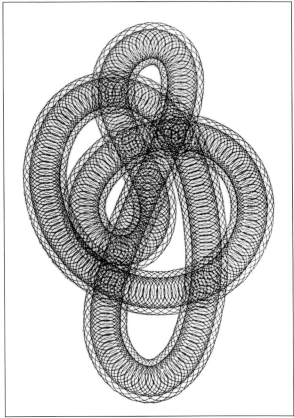

83
Ia. Chernikhov, *Ornament.*
Classically Composed
Structures, 1931, p.185:
diagrams 607, 608
(C.185.bb.10).

84
N. Punin, *New Tendencies*
in Russian Art, 1927, cover
with reproduction of
Fishermen by V. Tatlin
(Cup.408.d.23).

they are vague. The verdict must surely be that Chernikhov's almost unlimited
imagination for architectural forms provides a pattern book for modernist
architecture, rather than a repertoire of viable designs.

In *Style and Epoch* Ginzburg had attempted to define a new style, but
(writing in 1923) had concluded that adverse economic conditions had prevented
enough building to assess its virtues and shortcomings. By the early 1930s, when
there were plenty of examples of completed buildings reproduced in books and
journals – including Lissitzky's well-illustrated study of Russian architecture,
published in German in 1930[72] – the impediment no longer existed. But a second
strand in Ginzburg's argument was his definition of three stages of a style, of
which the final was 'decorative', and Chernikhov's buildings seem to illustrate
this phase. It is remarkable that only six years should elapse between the
publication of Ginzburg's prediction and its fulfilment, albeit in books with
immense charm, written by an architect who continued his work as a valued
teacher, and whose influence was more acceptable than that of his extremist
colleagues.

Very little has been said here about the development of fine art
through the 1920s. This is because of the preference of most avant-garde artists in
the 1920s for architecture and design – whether they designed furniture or books.
The two main groups of Realist painters, members of the pre-Revolutionary
group, the Wanderers (*Peredvizhniki*) and the new group formed in May 1922,

НОВЕЙШИЕ ТЕЧЕНИЯ
в
РУССКОМ ИСКУССТВЕ

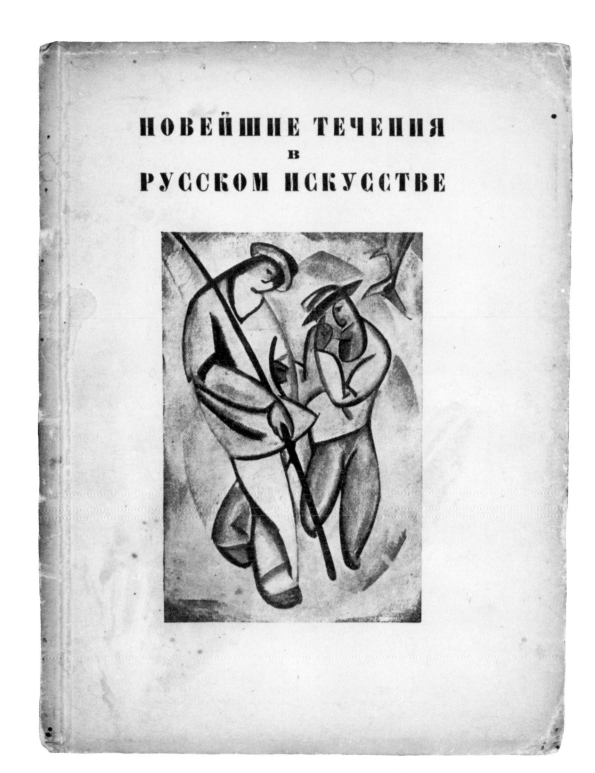

under the title the Association of Artists of Revolutionary Russia (*AKhRR*),[73] did not work on books in spite of success in obtaining commissions for easel paintings. Only towards the end of the decade were several books on painting with interesting covers published in Leningrad by the Russian Museum. They chronicle the general change-over towards a more representational art form: a wash-drawing of *Fishermen* by Tatlin, resurrected from around 1912, is reproduced on the cover [84] of a pamphlet by Punin entitled *New Tendencies in Russian Art (Noveishie techeniia v russkom iskusstve)* issued by the Museum secretariat in 1927; a second volume by the same author carries a photograph of a painting of a woodland scene by Lev Bruni.[74] The following year the Museum published the exhibition catalogue, *Workers' Art (Iskusstvo rabochikh)*;[75] on its cover [85] the title is written in blue letters forming a square which is superimposed on a plain black one. The designer is given as 'M. Brodsky' who used a style defiantly reminiscent of Suprematism. Tugendkhold, who had championed avant-garde artists such as Ekster and Chagall with his monographs of the first post-Revolutionary years, was by 1930 reflecting the new climate of artistic opinion in his choice of artists. His *Art of the October Epoch (Iskusstvo oktiabr'skoi epokhi)*[76] has a stylish but old-fashioned cover, designed in red and black by Dmitry Mitrokhin, a former member of Diaghilev's *World of Art* group. In its own way, however, even this could be considered Formalist and was destined to be condemned with the middle-of-the-road painters, sculptors and graphic artists – including Petrov-Vodkin – whose work was reproduced in the book. It is not surprising that fine-art books were a low priority for writers and designers alike, for it was a simple matter for the authorities to exercise immediate control over easel painting, drawings and book design. After 1932 criticism was extended to artists who had been leaders shortly after the Revolution and Osip Beskin's *Formalism in Painting (Formalizm v zhivopisi)*[77] included reproductions of work by Shterenberg – once Lunacharsky's trusted head of *IZO* – as well as more obvious targets such as Pavel Filonov – whose retrospective in Leningrad had been prevented from opening.[78]

When rigid censorship was imposed in 1934 the design of books was affected forthwith. None the less, the imaginative designs reproduced in these pages provide a taste of the very large number of avant-garde books and journals produced in the Soviet Union in the 1920s. They could not be destroyed or suppressed and have provided a record of that Russian art and architecture which has, over the past few decades, increasingly taken its rightful place in the history of twentieth-century art.[79] Modern developments in printing techniques have resulted in the widespread use of colour reproductions on the covers of books about art and architecture, yet these rarely match the distinguished designs produced under less favourable conditions between 1917 and 1934.

86
LEF, No.1, 1923, cover by
A. Rodchenko
(C.104.dd.51).

Notes

1 The 1920s and 1930s

1 The poster is reproduced in Sergei Esenin, *Selected Poetry*, transl. from Russian by Peter Tempest, Moscow 1982. Details of literary groups are given in *Handbook of Russian Literature*, ed. by Victor Terras, New Haven/London, 1985.

2 See *Changing Attitudes in Soviet Russia. The Family in the USSR: Documents and Readings*, ed. by Rudolf Schlesinger, London 1949, pp.281-2 and pp.30,33.

3 *McGraw-Hill Encyclopedia of Russia and the Soviet Union*, ed. by Michael T. Florinsky, New York and London 1961, pp.150-1.

4 Such posters are reproduced in colour in *Soviet Commercial Design of the Twenties*, ed. by Mikhail Anikst, intro. by Elena Chernevich; transl. from Russian and ed. by Catherine Cooke, London 1987, pp.48-9.

5 Stepanova is seen modelling the cap in photographs reproduced in Alexander Lavrentiev, *Varvara Stepanova: A Constructivist Life*, transl. from Russian by Wendy Salmond, ed. by John E. Bowlt, London 1988, p.111.

6 B. Irkutov and Nikulin, *Vecher knigi*, Moscow: Krasnaia nov', 1924. Cover reproduced in Lavrentiev 1988 (see previous note), p.114.

7 The dramatic evening was directed by Vitalii Zhemchuzhnyi at the Akademiia kommunisticheskogo vospitaniia im. N. K. Krupskoi using the drama, artistic and choral society of the Komsomol. An article by Brik and four production photographs are reproduced in *LEF* No.1, 1925; also in Lavrentiev 1988 (see note 5), pp.112-15.

8 'Throw Pushkin, Dostoevskii, Tolstoi, et al. overboard from the ship of modernity', from the manifesto 'A Slap in the Face of Public Taste' signed by D. Burliuk, Kruchenykh, Maiakovskii and Khlebnikov and translated in Vladimir Markov, *Russian Futurism, A History*, London 1969, p.45-6

9 Accounts of these books are given in Susan Compton, *The World Backwards: Russian Futurist Books 1912-16*, London 1978 (the companion volume to this study) and in Susan Compton, *Domarsumpen* [A Trap for Judges], Stockholm 1983 (in Swedish); Gerald Janecek, *The Look of Russian Literature: Avant-Garde Visual Experiments, 1900-1930*, New Jersey 1984; Evgenii Kovtun, *Russkaia futuristicheskaia kniga*, Moscow 1989, and 'Experiments in Book Design by Russian Artists', *The Journal of Decorative and Propaganda Arts* 5, 1987, pp.46-59.

10 See the bibliography and references in the notes for numerous studies which have provided invaluable material.

11 Sheila Fitzpatrick, *The Commissariat of Enlightenment: Soviet Organisation of Education and the Arts under Lunacharsky, October 1917-21*, Cambridge 1970, p.120, cited from B. F. Malkin, in *V. Maiakovskii v vospominaniiakh sovremennikov*, Moscow 1963, p.635.

12 Nikolai Punin, article in *Zhizn' iskusstva*, No.816, 8 Nov. 1921, p.1, cited as 'In the days of Red October', in Fitzpatrick 1970 (see note 11) p.122.

13 *Makovets: zhurnal iskusstv*, No.1, No.2, 1922 (Cup.408.h.1). No.2 was published in memory of the artist Vasilii Nikolaevich Chekrygin who was run over by a train on 3 June 1922. See Troels Andersen and Ksenia Grigorieva, *Art et poésie russes 1900-1930: textes choisis*, ed. by Olga Makhroff and Stanislas Zadora, Paris 1979, pp.192-9. Information about the other groupings is given in Alan Bird, *A History of Russian Painting*, Oxford 1987, and Christina Lodder, *Russian Constructivism*, New Haven and London 1983. The Four Arts group is discussed in detail in Peter Stupples, *Pavel Kuznetsov: his Life and Art*, Cambridge 1989, chapter 17.

14 Kuz'ma Sergeevich Petrov-Vodkin, *Samarkandiia: iz putevykh nabroskov 1921g.* Petersburg: Akvilon, 1923 (September) (X.705/667).

15 *Russkoe iskusstvo*, No.1 and No.2-3, Moscow/Petersburg 1923 (PP.1931.pmh).

16 Compton 1978 (see note 9).

17 Larionov and Goncharova also provided illustrations for: V. Ia. Parnakh, *L'Art Décoratif Théâtral Moderne*, Paris 1919, (11795.tt.2); V. Ia. Parnakh, *Motdinamo, (Slovodvig)*, Paris, Editions La Cible, 1920, (C.135.g.9) and A. Blok, *Dvenadtsat'. Skify*, Paris 1920 (Cup.408.g.26); Larionov for A. Blok, *The Twelve*, London 1920 (Cup.408.g.27); and Goncharova for V. Ia. Parnakh, *Samum*, Paris 1919, (C.114.mm.13) and A. S. Pushkin, *Conte de Tsar Saltan et de son fils le glorieux et puissant Prince Guidon Saltanovitch et de la belle Princesse Cygne*, transl. by Claude Anet, Paris, La Sirène, 1921 (C.114.mm.10).

18 David Burliuk continued publishing activities in New York with his wife Marussiia, often including reminiscences of Hylaea: D. D. Burliuk, *Stikhi i biografiia*, New York 1924, (C.104.d.39); *Manifesto Radio-style*, [New York] 1926, (C.185.bb.6); *Marusia-san*, New York: Izdatel'stvo "Shag", 1925 (C.185.b.7); *Krasnaia strela: sbornik-antologiia*, New York: izd. Marii Burliuk, 1932, (C.185.bb.9); *Polovina veka (izdano k piatidesiatiletiiu so dnia rozhdeniia poeta)*, [New York]: Izdatel'stvo Marii N. Burliuk, [1932] (C.185.bb.8).

19 V.V. Maiakovskii, *Solntse: poema*, Moscow/Petersburg: Krug, 1923 (C.114.mm.15).

20 M.O. Tsetlin (Amari), *Prozrachnye teni: obrazy*, Paris/Moscow: K-vo "Zerna", 1920 (May) (Cup.408.i.20).

21 A full discussion of the origins of Constructivism is given in Lodder 1983 (see note 13).

22 K.S. Malevich, *Ot Sezanna do suprematizma: kriticheskii ocherk*, Moscow: Otdel Izobrazitel'nykh Iskusstv Narkomprosa, [1920] (C.114.m.34).

23 N.N. Punin, *Tatlin: protiv kubizma*, Petrograd 1921 (C.145.a.2).

24 V.V. Maiakovskii, *Vladimir Maiakovskii – Tragediia*, Moscow 1914 (C.114.mm.4).

25 V. Khlebnikov and others, *Moskovskie mastera: zhurnal iskusstv*, Moscow, 1916 (Spring) (C.114.mm.21).

26 *Strelets: sbornik pervyi*, ed. by A. Belenson, Petrograd, 1915 (C.106.f.13).

27 D. Burliuk, G. Zolotukhin, V.V. Kamenskii, and others, *Chetyre ptitsy: sbornik stikhov*, Moscow, 1916 (C.114.mm.26).

28 V.V. Kamenskii, *Sten'ka Razin: roman*, Moscow: Knigoizd-vo "K", 1916 (12589.s.9). One of Lentulov's vignettes is reproduced in E.B. Murina, S.G. Dzhafarova, *Aristarkh Lentulov*, Moscow 1990, p.212.

29 A. Belyi and others, in *Iav': stikhi*, Moscow, 1919 (Cup.403.w.19), p.24-9.

30 R. Ivnev, A. Mariengof, M. Roizman, V. Shershenevich, *Imazhinisty*, Moscow: Izdanie avtorov, 1925 (C.191.b.4).

31 S. Bobrov, *Vertogradari nad lozami*, Moscow, 1913 (C.114.n.35); the book is discussed in Compton 1978 (see note 9), p.75, where two colour lithographs by Goncharova are reproduced as plates 6 and 7.

32 *Tsentrifuga* No.2, ed. by S.P. Bobrov, Moscow: Tsentrifuga, 1916, 181 numbered copies, of which BL copy is No.6 (C.104.dd.5). The cover is reproduced in colour in Compton 1983 (see note 9), as colour plate viii; Bobrov's *Tsentrifuga* provided Markov with subject-matter for a whole chapter of his *Russian Futurism*, Markov 1969 (see note 8), pp.228-75.

33 S.P. Bobrov, *Lira lir: tret'ia kniga stikhov*, Moscow: Tsentrifuga, 1917 (Cup.408.i.15).

34 S.P. Bobrov, *Vosstanie mizantropov*, Moscow: Tsentrifuga, 1922 (Cup.408.d.35).

35 N.N. Aseev, *Zor*, Moscow: Liren', 1914 (printed in Kharkhov) (C.114.n.34, Mic.A.7632).

36 N.N. Aseev, G. Petnikov, and others, *Letorei*, 1915 (August) includes an unexplained blank page overprinted with a black rectangle; this was either a foretaste of Malevich's Suprematism (unveiled at the exhibition 0.10 in December 1915) or, more likely, inspired by a page from the eighteenth century English novel by Laurence Sterne, *Tristram Shandy*, which had been translated into Russian early in the nineteenth century and was a favourite of Russian linguists in the 1910s and of the Formalists in the 1920s: Sterne's original book features such a page.

37 Markov 1969 (see note 8), p.246; Markov also notes that Liren' published Khlebnikov's manifesto, *Truba Marsian*, signed also by Aseev and Maria Siniakova, as well as his play, *Oshibka smerti*, p.247.

38 A.E. Kruchenykh, G. Petnikov and V. Khlebnikov, *Zaumniki*, [Petrograd]: EUY, 1922 (C.114.n.37, Mic.A. 7632).

39 A.E. Kruchenykh, *Razboinik Van'ka-Kain i Son'ka-Manikiurshchitsa: ugolovnyi roman*, Moscow: izdanie Vserossiiskogo soiuza poetov, kniga 132-ia, 1925 (cover date 1926) (Cup.408.i.26).

40 N.N. Aseev, V.V. Maiakovskii, *Odna golova vsegda bedna, a potomu i bedna, chto zhivet odna*, Moscow: Kooperatsiia "Tsentral'noe tovarishchestvo", 1924 (C.114.mm.51); *Rasskaz o tom, putem kakim s bedoi upravilsia Akim*, Moscow: Tsentral'noe t-vo "Kooperativ izdatel'stvo", 1925 (C.114.mm.52); *Pervyi pervomai*, Leningrad: Rabochee izdatel'stvo, "Priboi", 1926 (Cup.408.i.4).

41 'Postanovlenie o Revoliutsionnom Tribunale Pechati', *Pravda*, 1 Jan.1918, cited in Ernest J. Simmons, 'The Origins of Literary Control', Part I, *Survey: A Journal of Soviet and East European Studies*, No.36, April-June 1961, pp.82-3.

42 Simmons, 'The Origins of Literary Control' Part II, *Survey* (as previous note) No.37, July-Sept. 1961, p.60.

43 Simmons 1961, (Part II), as previous note.

44 M. Shchelkunov, article in *Pechat' i revoliutsiia*, 1922, No.6, p.183, cited as 'Legislation on printing over five years', in Fitzpatrick 1970 (see note 11), p.133.

45 Fitzpatrick 1970 (see note 11), p.262.

46 The numbers of privately published books were 1919: 289, 1920: 122, given in Fitzpatrick 1970 (see note 11), p.263; information about new title numbers is given in Marc Slonim, 'The New Spirit in Russian Literature' in George Reavey and Marc Slonim, *Soviet Literature: An Anthology*, London 1933, p.17.

47 A. Lunacharski, [sic] *Self-education of the Workers. The Cultural Task of the Struggling Proletariat*, London: The Workers' Socialist Federation [1919], p.4.

48 For information on posters and technique see Nikolai Shkolnyi, 'Persuading the People: Posters of the First Soviet Years', in *Tradition and Revolution in Russian Art: Leningrad in Manchester*, exhibition catalogue, Manchester 1990, p.104.

49 V. Lebedev, *Russian Placards 1917-1922, 1st part*, Petersburg: Petersburg office of the Russian Telegraph Agency ROSTA, Strelets, 1923. (C.191.a.13) The book consists of a set of plates of poster designs by Lebedev introduced (in English): 'The series of placards reproduced in this book were executed by Wladimir Lebedeff for the show-windows of the Russian Telegraph Agency (ROSTA) in Petersburg for agitation purposes. The present edition is the first part of the series illustrating Russian placards, the second part will be published in a short time.'

50 Fitzpatrick 1970 (see note 11), p.264.

51 Fitzpatrick 1970 (see note 11), p.265.

52 Information from a meeting of the Press Section of the Central Committee, May 9-10 1924, in *K voprosu o politike RKP(b) v khudozhestvennoi literature*, Moscow 1924, pp.83-4; cited in English in Robert A. Maguire, *Red Virgin Soil: Soviet Literature in the 1920s*, Princeton 1968, p.9, n.17: journals published by Gosizdat included *Krasnaia Nov'*, *LEF* and *Oktiabr'*.

53 Maurice Friedberg,'Soviet Books, Censors and Readers', in *Literature and Revolution in Soviet Russia 1917-1962*, ed. by Max Hayward and Leopold Labedz, London 1963, p.198.

54 Fitzpatrick 1970 (see note 11), p.263.

55 Fitzpatrick 1970 (see note 11), p.264.

56 See Edward J. Brown, *The Proletarian Episode in Russian*

Literature, 1928-1932, New York 1953: he discusses the resolutions on pp.43-5; the document is translated in full as Appendix A, pp.235-40.

57 *Vsesoiuznaia Poligraficheskaia Vystavka: putevoditel'*, Moscow: Izdanie K-ta Vsesoiuznoi Poligraficheskoi Vystavki, 1927 (Nov.) (Cup.410.e.87).

58 *McGraw-Hill Encyclopedia 1961* (see note 3), p.455.

59 Brown 1953 (see note 56) discusses the resolutions on pp.88-9; the document is translated in full as Appendix B, pp.244–2.

60 O. Brik, 'The So-Called Formal Method', transl. by Ann Shukman, *Russian Poetics in Translation*, Vol.4, Oxford 1977, reprinted by Gerard Conio, Preface, transl. by Rupert Swyer, *The Futurists, the Formalists and the Marxist Critique*, ed. by Christopher Pike, London 1979, p.47-8.

61 A. Belyi, M. Gor'kii and others, *Kak my pishem*, Leningrad: Izdatel'stvo pisatelei v Leningrade, 1930 (11874.aa.9).

62 English translations in Louis Fischer, *Machines and Men in Russia*, New York 1932, Chapter XVI (10292.bbb.32).

63 Fischer 1932 (see previous note) p.240.

64 Fischer 1932 (see note 62) pp.243-8.

65 I. E. Babel', *Rasskazy*, Moscow: Federatsiia, 1932 (October), (12591.pp.44).

66 Friedberg, in Hayward and Labedz 1963 (see note 53), pp.198-9.

67 Brown 1953 (see note 56) quotes the resolution on pp.200-1.

68 Edward J. Brown, *Russian Literature Since the Revolution*, revised and enlarged edition, Cambridge, Mass. and London 1982, p.15.

69 All the quotations in the above paragraph are taken from Brown 1982 (see previous note), p.15.

70 Fischer 1932 (see note 51), p.233.

71 Fischer 1932 (see note 51), pp.239-40.

72 See *Problems of Soviet Literature*, ed. by H. G. Scott, London 1935, reprinted as *Soviet Writers' Congress, 1934: The Debate on Socialist Realism and Modernism in the Soviet Union*, London 1977.

73 Friedberg in Hayward and Labedz 1963 (see note 53), pp.199-200; Friedberg cites Glavlit order No.149 of 11 August 1935, from L. G. Fogelevich, *Osnovye direktivy i zakonodatel'stvo o pechati: sistematicheskii sbornik*, 5th edition, Moscow: Gosizdat "Sovetskoe zakonodatel'stvo", 1935, p.117; as this edition of Fogelevich was published in 1935 it seems to the present author more likely that the Order was of 1934; in correspondence with the author, Maurice Friedberg – being unable to check the source – agrees that 1935 is probably a misprint in his article. The order gave the censors the power to decide on the technical make-up of all books.

74 Friedberg in Hayward and Labedz 1963 (see note 53), p.199.

75 Dziga Vertov's film, *The Man with the Movie Camera*, was in production in 1928 and released in 1929. The high-contrast shots are compared with Rodchenko's photograph in Vlada Petrić, *Constructivism in Film: 'The Man with the Movie Camera', A Cinematographic Analysis*, Cambridge 1987, p.131.

76 Cited in German Karginov, *Rodchenko*, transl. from Hungarian by Elizabeth Hoch, London 1979, p.245.

77 Cited in Karginov 1979 (see previous note), p.245.

78 Cited in Karginov 1979 (see note 76), p.246.

79 For instance, Alexander Solzhenitsyn, *One Day in the Life of Ivan Denisovich*, London 1963, also, *The First Circle*, London 1968, and, amongst other writings, his three volumes on *The Gulag Archipelago 1918-1956*; Nadezhda Mandelstam, *Hope against Hope, a Memoir*, London 1970; Evgeniia Ginzburg, *Into the Whirlwind*, London 1967.

80 V. Shklovskii, *Moskva rekonstruiruetsia, al'bom diagramm, toposkhem i fotografii po rekonstruktsii gor. Moskvy*, ed. by G. M. Garfunkel', Moscow 1938 (L.R.274.d.30).

81 S. M. Tret'iakov, *Iasnysh: stikhi*, Moscow: Ptach, 1922; (20003.f.37); *Slyshish', Moskva? Agit-gin'ol' v 4-kh deistviiakh*, Moscow: Vserossiiskii proletkul't, 1924 (X.902/3151); *Itogo: stikhi*, Moscow: Gosudarstvennoe izdatel'stvo, 1924 (11588.h.27); *Svanetiia: ocherk iz knigi "V pereulkakh gor"*, (Bibliotechka "Rabochei Moskvy" No.14), Moscow: Izd. "Rabochaia", 1928 (010058.s.6); *Rechevik: stikhi*, predislovie I. Dukora, Moscow/Leningrad: Gosudarstvennoe izdatel'stvo, 1929 (011586.f.92); *Den Shi-khua: bio-interv'iu*, Moscow: Molodaia gvardiia, 1931 (July) (1067.cc.11).

82 See previous note.

83 See note 81.

84 Sume-Cheng, *Kitaianka Sume-Cheng/ Soumé Scheng, souvenirs d'enfance et de révolution*, transl. from French by E. S. Vaitinskii, Moscow/Leningrad, 1929 (YA.1989.a.14921). Seven thousand copies were printed.

85 Tret'iakov was arrested in 1939.

2 Writers and Designers: new partnerships

1 The exhibition was shown in Paris in 1975-6, see *Maiakovski, 20 ans de travail*, Centre national d'art et de culture, Georges Pompidou, Centre National d'art contemporain, (11 rue Berryer) and in Oxford in 1982, see *Mayakovsky, Twenty Years of Work: an Exhibition from the State Museum of Literature Moscow*, ed. by David Elliott, Oxford, 1982. A list of material exhibited is printed in the French catalogue.

2 D. Burliuk, A. Kruchenykh, V. Mayakovskii, V. Khlebnikov, and others, *Poshchechina obshchestvennomu vkusu*, Moscow, 1912 (C.105.a.4).

3 V. Maiakovskii, *Bez doklada ne vkhodit'*, Moscow, 1930 (C.127.d.22); Sergei Sen'kin's name is printed vertically along the edge of the cover photograph.

4 Edward J. Brown gives an account of Osip Brik's visit to Stalin which resulted in this verdict, in *Mayakovsky, A Poet in the Revolution*, Princeton 1973, pp.369-70. For Mayakovsky's gift to the Museum, see N. V. Shakhalova, 'The State Museum of Literature', *Mayakovsky, Thirty Years of Work* 1982 (see note 1), p.102.

5 See Bengt Jangfeldt, *Majakovskij and Futurism 1917-1921*, Stockholm 1977, p.35.

6 A. E. Kruchenykh, *15 let russkogo futurizma 1912-1927 gg.: materialy i kommentarii*, Moscow: Izdanie Vserossiiskogo soiuza poetov, 1928 (C.136.b.33).

7 Gordon McVay, 'Alexei Kruchenykh, The Bogeyman of Russian Literature', *Russian Literature Triquarterly*, No.13, Fall 1975. McVay's article is based on his interviews with Kruchenykh in Moscow in the 1960s.

8 On p.60 of *15 let russkogo futurizma* Kruchenykh says that he retired to the Caucasus; further details are given in Marzio Marzaduri, 'Futurismo Menscevico', *L'Avanguardia a Tiflis: studi, ricerche, cronache, testimonianze, documenti*, eds. Luigi

Magarotto, Marzio Marzaduri, Giovanna Pagani Cesa (Quaderni del seminario di iranistica, ural-altaistica e caucasologia, Vol.13), Venice: Universita degli studi di Venezia, 1982, p.109. The place Batalpachinsk was re-named Cherkessk in 1926 (map ref. 44.14N 42.05E); Sarikamis (map ref. 40.19N 42.35E), pronounced 'Sarukamush', is 20 kms from Kars, then joined to Tiflis by a railway line, shown on a sketch map in C. E. Bechhofer, *In Denikin's Russia and the Caucasus, 1919-1920*, London 1921, between pp.5 and 6. Sarikamis had been in Russian Armenia since 1878; Marzaduri states that Kruchenykh moved to Tiflis when the province of Kars was taken by the Turks.

9 A. E. Kruchenykh, *Uchites' khudogi*, Tiflis 1917 (C.114.n.43).

10 A. E. Kruchenykh, *1918*, Tiflis 1917.

11 Information on Il'ia Zdanevich and his University from *Iliazd*, exhibition catalogue, Centre Georges Pompidou, Paris 1978, pp.13-14, where the source is given as Zdanevich's 1922 notes.

12 Kruchenykh later printed lists of his books at the back of each new title; among those produced in Tiflis the following titles are held by the British Library: *Uchites' khudogi*, Tiflis 1917, (C.114.n.43, microfilm A 7632); *Ozhirenie roz: o stikhakh Terent'eva i drugikh*, [Tiflis 1919?] (C.104.dd.7); *Malakholiia v kapote*, Tiflis, 1918 (Cup.410.b.108, No.12 of 50 copies); *Lakirovannoe triko*, Tiflis: Tipografiia Soiuza gorodov Respubliki Gruzii, 1919 (C.114.m.23).

13 *Sofii Georgievne Mel'nikovoi, Fantasticheskii kabachok*, Tiflis, 41°, 1919 (Sept.) (C.104.dd.6).

14 Grigory Robak'idze, 'Kartuli mts'erloba', *Phalestra*: undated quotation transl. in T. Nikolskaya, 'Russian Writers in Georgia in 1917-1921', *The Ardis Anthology of Russian Futurism*, ed. by Ellendea Proffer and Carl R. Proffer, Ann Arbor 1980, p.301.

15 Eli Eganbiuri (pseudonym for Il'ia Zdanevich), *Nataliia Goncharova, Mikhail Larionov*, Moscow: 1913 (C.114.mm.22).

16 See note 12.

17 I. Terent'ev, *Fakt*, Tiflis: 41°, 1919 (C.114.r.5).

18 The information is printed in A. Kruchenykh, *Fonetika teatra*, Moscow: 41°, 1923 (12975.b.25).

19 Vladimir Markov, *Russian Futurism: A History*, London 1969, p.330.

20 V. V. Kamenskii, *Ego-moia biografiia velikogo futurista*, Moscow: Knigoizd-vo Kitovras, 1918 (X.981/12542: the BL copy lacks the portraits mentioned by Markov).

21 V. V. Kamenskii, *Tango s korovami*, Moscow 1914 (C.114.n.32). Kamenskii's poems are reproduced in Gerald Janecek, *The Look of Russian Literature: Avant-Garde Visual Experiments, 1900-1930*, Princeton 1984, figs.112-18, pp.159-63.

22 V. V. Kamenskii, *Saryn' na kichku*, Moscow: Federatsiia, 1932 (C.191.a.16); V. V. Kamenskii, *Iunost' Maiakovskogo*, [Tiflis] Zakkniga, 1931 (Cup.408.d.37).

23 V. V. Maiakovskii, *Chelovek, Veshch'*, [Moscow], Izd. ASIS, [1918] (C.114.mm.11); *Oblako v shtanakh: Tetraptikh*, [Moscow] Izd. ASIS, [1918] (Cup.408.d.51). Before the establishment of ASIS Maiakovskii had published a book with Parus, the firm run by Maxim Gorkii: V. V. Maiakovskii, *Voina i mir*, Petrograd, Parus, 1917 (C.127.d.23).

24 *Gazeta futuristov*, single issue March 1918. For a discussion of the paper and its finance by Lev Grinkrug, see Bengt Jangfeldt, *Majakovskij and Futurism 1917-1921*, Stockholm 1977, p.17 ff. Jangfeldt's thesis provides useful information on these early post-Revolutionary years.

25 Information about the Creation Group is from Jangfeldt 1977 (see note 24), pp.108-17.

26 'Manifest letuchei federatsii futuristov' is printed (in Russian) in Jangfeldt 1977 (see note 24), pp.20-2.

27 Revoliutsiia dukha is treated fully in Jangfeldt 1977 (see note 24), pp.65-9. The spiritual side of revolutionary change can be seen in 1922, when *Makovets: zhurnal iskusstv*, Nos. 1 and 2 (Cup.408.h.1) were published. On the title 'Makovets' see John E. Bowlt, *Russian Art of the Avant-Garde: Theory and Criticism 1902-1934*, New York 1976, p.300, note 47.

28 Peter Stupples, *Pavel Kuznetsov: his Life and Art*, Cambridge 1989, pp.181-2.

29 *Anarkhiia* was published by the Federation of Moscow Anarchist Groups from February to April 1918 from their headquarters, Anarchy House (the former Merchants Club) with the Poets' Cafe; among contributors were K. Malevich, V. Tatlin, A. Gan, A. Rodchenko, N. Punin and A. Lourié. The last issue, No.45, came out on 24 April after the forcible closure of Anarchy House on 12 April 1918; as the Poets' Cafe was closed two days later Andersen believes the two were closely linked. See Troels Andersen and Ksenia Grigorieva, *Art et poésie russes 1900-1930, textes choisis*, ed. by Olga Makhroff and Stanislas Zadora, Paris 1979, pp.107-8.

30 K. Malevich, 'Arkhitektura kak poshchechina betona-zhelezu,' *Anarkhiia*, No.37, April 6 1918, was reprinted in *Iskusstvo kommuny*, No.1, December 7 1918; English transl. in *Malevich, Essays on Art 1915-1933*, Vol.1, ed. by Troels Andersen, transl. by Xenia Glowacki-Prus and Arnold McMillin, London 1968, pp.60-4. *Iskusstvo kommuny*, Petrograd: Izdanie Otdela Izobrazitel'nykh Iskusstv Komissariata Narodnogo Prosveshcheniia: nineteen issues were published between 7 December 1918 and 13 April 1919 (C.191.c.6). The BL holding lacks Nos 2, 13, 17.

31 For *Iskusstvo kommuny*, see previous note. *Iskusstvo: vestnik Otdela Izobrazitel'nykh Iskusstv Narodnogo Komissariata po Prosveshcheniiu*, Moscow 1919. It appeared eight times between January and December 1919.

32 See the chronology in *Vladimir Mayakovsky: Innovator*, transl. from Russian by Alex Miller, Moscow 1976, p.287.

33 Quoted in 'Khronika sovetskoi literatury za 20 let', *Literaturnyi kritik*, No.7, 1937, pp.139-40; cited in English in E. J. Simmons, 'Origins of Literary Control', Part II, *Survey, A Journal of Soviet and East European Studies*, No.37, July-Sept. 1961, p.63.

34 Information about IMO from O. Brik, *IMO – Iskusstvo molodykh*, Leningrad 1940, p.100, cited in Jangfeldt 1977 (see note 24), p.128, n.2.

35 V. V. Maiakovskii, *Vse sochinennoe Vladimirom Maiakovskim 1909-1919*, Petersburg: IMO, 1919 (011586.l.73).

36 V. V. Maiakovskii, *Rzhanoe slovo*, Moscow, IMO, 1918. The word 'rzhanoi', literally 'rye' acquired connotations of 'simple', 'peasant' and 'Russian' and became almost synonymous with 'new' (novoe) in 1918, according to Charles Rougle, 'National and International in Majakovskij', *Vladimir Majakovskij, Memoirs and Essays*, ed. by Bengt Jangfeldt and Nils Åke Nilsson, (Stockholm Studies in

Russian Literature 2), Stockholm 1975, p.191.

37 Jangfeldt 1977 (see note 24), p.128, n.2 (as note 36 above).

38 December 22, 1918. Jangfeldt 1977 (see note 24), gives an account of Kom-Fut: pp.94-108; he gives the manifesto in Russian, pp.98-9.

39 *Izobraziteľnoe iskusstvo*, Petersburg: Narkompros, 1919 (L.R.416.tt.10).

40 N. N. Punin, *Pamiatnik III Internatsionala: proekta khud. V.E.Tatlina*, Petersburg: Izdanie Otdela Izobraziteľnykh Iskusstv N.K.P., 1920 (7823.d.37).

41 For instance, in *MA*, May, 1922; *Zenit*, October, 1922; *Merz*, April-July 1924.

42 TsGALI, fond 681, op.1, ed. by khr.1018,1.196: cited by Stupples 1989 (see note 28), p.198.

43 Quotations from A.Bogdanov, 'Puti proletarskogo tvorchestva', *Proletarskaia kuľtura*, No.15/16, 1920, pp.50-2, English transl. in Bowlt 1976 (see note 27), pp.178-82.

44 'Khronika', *Literaturnyi kritik*, No.8, 1920, p.103 cited in Edward J.Brown, *The Proletarian Episode in Russian Literature 1928-1932*, New York 1953, p.9.

45 'Proletkuľt', *Literaturnaia entsiklopediia*, IX, 1935, pp.309-10, cited in Brown 1953 (see previous note), p.9.

46 For Gastev and his poetry see Kathleen Lewis and Harry Weber, 'Zamiatin's *We*, The Proletarian Poets and Bogdanov's *Red Star*', *The Ardis Anthology of Russian Futurism*, ed. by Ellendea Proffer and Carl R.Proffer, Ann Arbor 1980, pp.259-65.

47 A short account of Taylor and his ideas is given by Frank Barkley Copley, 'Frederick W.Taylor: Revolutionist' in Frederick W.Taylor, *Two Papers on Scientific Management: A Piece-rate System and Notes on Belting*, London 1919; Taylor's best-known book is his *Principles of Scientific Management*, New York/London 1911.

48 See Hugh G.J.Aitken, *Taylorism at Watertown Arsenal: Scientific Management in Action 1908-15*, Cambridge Mass., 1960. Piece work was still in operation in the Soviet Union in 1931, see Louis Fischer, *Machines and Men in Russia*, New York 1932, pp.160-1.

49 A.V.Lunacharskii,'Ocherki russkoi literatury revoliutsionnogo vremeni', in A.V.Lunacharskii, *Neizdannye materialy*, (Literaturnoe nasledstvo, Vol.82), ed. by R.Shcherbina, Moscow 1970, p.235; cited in Lewis and Weber 1980 (see note 46), p.258.

50 A.Gastev, 'O tendentsiiakh proletarskoi kuľtury', *Proletarskaia kuľtura*, No.9/10, 1919; cited in English by Lewis and Weber 1980 (see note 46), p.259.

51 A.Lunacharski, [sic] *Self-education of the Workers; The Cultural Task of the Struggling Proletariat*, London, The Workers' Socialist Federation (1919).

52 Jangfeldt 1977 (see note 24), p.102.

53 *Gorn*: literaturno-khudozhestvennyi i obshchestvenno-nauchnyi zhurnal, Kniga 8, Moscow: Izdanie Vserossiiskogo i Moskovskogo proletkuľtov, 1923 (PP.4842).

54 German Karginov, *Rodchenko*, transl. from Hungarian by Elisabeth Hoch, London 1979, p.194; the title page and two designs are reproduced in *Von der Malerei zum Design: Russische konstruktivistische Kunst der Zwanziger Jahre/From Painting to Design, Russian Constructivist Art of the Twenties*, exhibition catalogue, Galerie Gmurzynska, Cologne 1981, pp.280-2.

55 Frederik Uinslou Teilor, *Nauchnaia organizatsiia truda*, preface by P.M.Kerzhentseva, Moscow: Transpechat' 1925; a list of publications designed by Rodchenko and Stepanova is given in A.Lavrent'ev, *A.M.Rodchenko, V.F.Stepanova*, (Mastera sovetskogo knizhnogo iskusstva), Moscow 1989, p.149.

56 Book covers for Transpechat' by Rodchenko (and Stepanova) are reproduced in Lavrent'ev 1989 (see previous note) figs. 39-42; Lavrent'ev also reproduces Rodchenko's logo for Transpechat' as fig.38.

57 Memoirs of Galina Chichigova, a student at *VKhUTEMAS* in 1920, quoted in Karginov 1979 (see note 54), p.168.

58 A.Duglas, *Kak ustroit' kristallicheskii radiopriemnik i vse ego prinadlezhnosti*, Moscow: Transpechat' 1925; listed in Lavrent'ev 1989 (see note 55), p.149.

59 John Willett, *The New Sobriety, Art and Politics in the Weimar Period 1917-33*, London 1982, includes a discussion of the arts in Russia and Europe and interactions between the various countries, particularly between Germany and Russia.

60 V.V.Maiakovskii, *13 let raboty*, [Moscow]: MAF, 1922, 2 vols. (C.133.b.15).

61 George Grosz, *Mit Pinsel und Schere, 7 Materialisationen*, 1922. The cover is reproduced in Arturo Schwarz, *Almanacco Dada, antologia letteraria-artistica, Cronologia Repertorio delle riviste*, Milan 1976, p.538.

62 Willet 1982 (see note 59), chronology p.238; on p.83 Willet also cites a statement by Grosz and others, published in ?June 1921 in Herzfelde's *Der Gegner* No.8/9, calling for a new objectivity in place of aesthetic formulas. This appears to be contemporary with or even anticipate discussions on 'Veshchism' at Inkhuk mentioned below in Chapter 5.

63 For a full account of the spread of information about Russian art in Hungarian journals see Krystina Passuth, 'Contacts between the Hungarian and Russian Avant-Garde in the 1920s', *The First Russian Show. A Commemoration of the van Diemen Exhibition Berlin 1922*, exhibition catalogue, Annely Juda Fine Art, London 1983, pp.48-66; the cover of *Egység* No.1, Vienna, May 1922 is reproduced on p.49 but with the wrong year – 1921 – in the caption; Kossuth gives 1922 as the date in her text.

64 I.G.Erenburg, *A vse taki ona vertitsia*, Moscow/Berlin: Gelikon, 1922 (Jan.) (C.145.b.14).

65 *Veshch'/Gegenstand/Objet, révue internationale de l'art moderne*, ed. by El Lissitzky and I.G.Erenburg, Berlin: Skythen, No.1/2, March-April 1922, No.3, May 1922, (Cup.408.g.25).

66 Lissitzky designed the cover for and edited with Erenburg a single number of *Zenit*, No.17/18 Belgrade, Zagreb, 18 October 1922; and, with Hans Richter and Werner Graff, 'G', *Zeitschrift für Elementare Gestaltung*, Berlin, No.1 July and No.2, Sept. 1923; he designed and, with Kurt Schwitters, edited *Merz 8/9 Nasci*, Hanover, April-June 1924; he designed the covers for *Wendingen*, Vol.4 No.11, 1921 (published late summer, early autumn 1922), Amsterdam and Santpoort; he designed the cover of *MA, Aktivista folyóirat*, Vol.7 No.8, August 1922, Vienna; and *ABC, Beitrage zum Bauen*, Basel, 1924-1928. In 1922 he also designed covers for the American journal, *BROOM*.

67 Andrei B.Nakov, 'This Last exhibition which was the "First"', and Peter Nisbet, 'Some Facts on the Organizational History of the van Diemen Exhibition' in *The First Russian Show, 1983* (see note 63).

68 *Erste Russische Kunstaustellung*, exhibition catalogue, Galerie van Diemen, Berlin 1922 (Cup.410.f.119).

69 A letter from Maiakovskii to Chuzhak written after an editorial meeting of *LEF* on 22 Jan. 1923 is translated in Wiktor Woroszylski, *The Life of Mayakovsky*, transl. from Polish by Boleslaw Taborski, London 1972, pp.314-5.

70 *LEF: zhurnal levogo fronta iskusstv*, No.1 March, Moscow: Gosizdat 1923; No.2, April/May, Petrograd, Gosizdat, 1923 (BL holds Nos. 1 and 2 only (C.104.dd.51)). See note 80 below for details of further issues.

71 O.Brik, 'Ne poputchitsa', *LEF*, No.1, 1923 , p.109 ff. (C.104.dd.51); O.Brik, *Ne poputchitsa*, Moscow/Petrograd: Gosudarstvennoe izdatel'stvo, 1923 (Cup.408.g.24).

72 V.V.Maiakovskii, 'Pro eto', *LEF*, No.1, 1923, p.65 ff. V.V.Maiakovskii, *Pro eto*, Moscow/Petrograd: Gosizdat, 1923 (C.131.k.12).

73 See Gail Harrison Roman, *Ex Libris 6: Constructivism and Futurism: Russian and Other*, New York 1977, cat.32; Lavinskii's name is misprinted as 'Alavinskii'.

74 A quote from Trotskii's *Literatura i revoliutsiia*, 1923, cited in English in Gleb Struve, *Russian Literature under Lenin and Stalin 1917-1953*, Oklahoma 1971, p.76.

75 Posters by Maiakovskii and Rodchenko are reproduced in colour in *Soviet Commercial Design of the Twenties*, ed. by Mikhail Anikst, introduction by Elena Chernevich; transl. and ed. by Catherine Cooke, London 1987, pp.46-7.

76 5000 copies of *LEF* Nos. 1 and 2 of March and April-May 1923 were printed; 3000 of the next three, of June-July 1923, August-December 1923, and No.1. 1924; 2000 of the sixth, No 2, 1924, and 1500 of the seventh, No.3, 1925; information in *Ex Libris 6*, 1977 (see note 73), cat.154.

77 See Alexander Ushakov, 'Two destinies: Mayakovsky and George Grosz – Their Attitude to the Revolution', in the collection of essays by various authors, *Vladimir Mayakovsky: Innovator*, transl. by Alex Miller, Moscow 1976, p.186.

78 *L'art décoratif et industriel de l'U.R.S.S Moscou-Paris* 1925; the cover is reproduced in Lavrent'ev 1989 (see note 55), fig.36.

79 Rodchenko's silver medal award certificate for books is reproduced in *Alexander Rodtschenko und Warwara Stepanowa*, exhibition catalogue, Wilhelm-Lehmbruck-Museum der Stadt, Duisburg and Staatliche Kunsthalle Baden-Baden 1982, p.248.

80 V.V.Maiakovskii, *Parizh*, [Moscow]: Moskovskii rabochii, 1925 (C.136.b.29).

81 V.V.Maiakovskii, *Sergeiu Eseninu*, Tiflis: Zakkniga, 1926 (April) (1875.d.6(177)).

82 Sergei Esenin, *Kliuchi Marii*, Moscow: Izdatel'stvo Moskovskoi trudovoi arteli khudozhnikov slova, 1920, pp.15 and 19, cited in English and discussed by Viacheslav Zavalishin, *Early Soviet Writers*, New York 1958, p.119.

83 Zavalishin 1958 (see previous note), p.133; Imaginism is characterized on his pp.133-4.

84 R.Ivnev, A.B.Mariengof, M.Roizman, V.Shershenevich, *Imazhinisty*, Moscow: Izdanie avtorov, 1925 (C.191.b.4).

85 Books about Esenin by A.E.Kruchenykh are: *Liki Esenina: ot kheruvima do khuligana* (YA.1991.a.27653); *Esenin i Moskva kabatskaia, Liubov' khuligana, Dve avtobiografii Esenina* (C.191.a.15); *Khuligan Esenin* (11872.pp.15); *Novyi Esenin, o pervom tome Sobraniia stikhotvorenniia*; *Gibel' Esenina: kak Esenin prishel k samoubiistvu* (C.191.a.14); *Chornaia taina Esenina* (C.136.b.31); all published by the author, Moscow: 1926. The covers of all six are reproduced in Andersen and Grigorieva 1979 (see note 29), pp.281 and 282.

86 Cited from G.Gorbachov, *Sovremennaia russkaia literatura*, (2nd ed. revised and enlarged), Leningrad, 1929, in Struve 1971 (see note 74), p.26.

87 The back and front covers are reproduced in Lavrent'ev 1989 (see note 55), fig.90, with the variant back cover, a montage of a foal spotlit against a ladder-like structure, fig.91.

88 *Novyi LEF* (Novyi levyi front iskusstv – New Left Front of the Arts) 1927-8, 24 issues. BL holdings: No.5 May, No.6 June, and No.7 July, Moscow: Gosizdat, 1927 (C.104.dd.51). The covers of No.1 Jan.; No.3 March; No.4 April; No.7 July; No.8/9 August-Sept.; No.10 October; No.11/12 Nov.-Dec.(all 1927) are reproduced in *Ex Libris 6*, 1977 (see note 73), cat.209. Monthly issues of *Novyi LEF* continued until the end of 1928.

89 *Literatura fakta: pervyi sbornik materialov rabotnikov LEF'a*, ed by N.Chuzhak, Moscow, 1929 (11858.bbb.4).

90 The contents of *Literatura fakta* are discussed in Struve 1971 (see note 74), pp.215-7.

91 Maiakovskii's speech and an account of the evening is given in Woroszylski 1972 (see note 69), p.472-3.

92 See further p.28 above (Introduction). The Resolution is translated in full as Appendix B in Brown 1953 (see note 44), pp.241-2.

93 See note 1 above.

94 See E.J.Brown, 'The Year of Acquiescence', *Literature and Revolution in Soviet Russia 1917-62*, ed. by Max Hayward and Leopold Labedz, London 1963, pp.48-9.

95 Maiakovskii's suicide note is quoted in English in Woroszylski 1972 (see note 69), p.526.

96 P.Neznamov, (pseud. of Pavel Vasilevich Lezhankin) *Khorosho na ulitse*, Moscow: Federatsiia, 1929 (Cup.408.d.34).

97 Reproduced in Selim O.Khan-Magomedov, *Rodchenko: The Complete Works*, ed. by Vieri Quilici, transl. from Italian by Huw Evans, London 1986, p.107.

98 S.Tret'iakov, *Itogo: stikhi*. Moscow: Gosudarstvennoe izdatel'stvo, 1924 (11588.h.27).

99 A.Chicherin, E.-K.Sel'vinskii, K.Zelinskii, *Mena vsekh: konstruktivisty poety*, Moscow: Gosizdat, 1924, details in *Ex Libris 6*, 1977 (see note 73), cat.257.

100 *LEF* No.3, 1925: the signatories, Kornelii Zelinskii, Il'ia Sel'vinskii, Boris Agapov, Evgenii Gabrilovich and Vera Inber formed the Literary Centre of Constructivists (LTsK) in 1924. For an account of LTsK see Gail Weber, 'Constructivism and Soviet Literature', *Soviet Union* 3, pt 2, 1976, p.294-310.

101 O.Brik, and others, *Iskusstvo v proizvodstve: sborniki Khudozhestvenno-Proizvodstvennogo Soveta Otdela Izobrazitel'nykh Iskusstv Narkomprosa*, Vol.I, Moscow 1921 (Cup.410.d.80).

102 B.I.Arvatov, *Iskusstvo i klassy*, Moscow/Petrograd: Gosudarstvennoe Izdatel'stvo, 1923 (X.410/6110).

103 *Mena vsekh* 1924 (see note 99), p.24; cited in English in
D. G. B. Piper, *V. A. Kaverin, a Soviet Writer's Response to the
Problem of Commitment* (Duquesne Studies, Philological
Series), Duquesne 1971, p.40.

104 *Mena vsekh*, p.7; references as previous note.

105 M. I. Shchelkunov, *Istoriia, tekhnika, iskusstvo
knigopechatanniia*, Moscow/Leningrad: Gosudarstvennoe
izdatel'stvo, 1926, p.423 (2705.a.11).

106 Anri Barbius, *Rechi bortsa*, Moscow/Leningrad: Gosizdat,
1924.

107 *Gosplan literatury: sbornik*, ed. by K. L. Zelinskii and Il'ia
L. Sel'vinskii, [Moscow]: Literaturnyi tsentr
Konstruktivistov, 1925 (Cup.408.g.33).

108 1928 was characterized by congresses on literature which
are discussed in detail in Brown 1953 (see note 44),
especially pp.88-90.

109 *Izvestiia LTsK*, 1925 (August) (Cup.408.g.33). Front page
reproduced in *Ex Libris 6*, 1977 (see note 73), cat.93.

110 I. Sel'vinskii, *Zapiski poeta*, Moscow/Leningrad: Gikhl, 1928
(Cup.410.f.69).

111 I. L. Sel'vinskii, *Ulialaevshchina: epopeia*, Moscow: Krug, 1927
(11595.c.53). The plot is described in Zavalishin 1958 (see
note 82), pp.260-2.

112 A sample of checked flannel produced to a design by
Stepanova is reproduced in Alexander Lavrentiev, *Varvara
Stepanova: A Constructivist Life*, transl. from Russian by
Wendy Salmon, ed. by John E. Bowlt, London 1988, p.90.

113 *Biznes*, ed. by K. L. Zelinskii and I. L. Sel'vinskii, Moscow:
Gosizdat, 1929 (12349.s.18). Gail Weber 1976 (see note 100),
p.298, suggests that the cover is by Telingater; Gail Harrison
Roman, *Ex Libris 6*, 1977 (see note 73), cat.22, attributes it to
Rodchenko. The British Library copy lacks the paper cover.

114 K. L. Zelinskii, *Biznes* (see previous note), p.44; quoted in
English in Piper (see note 103), p.37.

115 Much space in the journal *Sovremennaia arkhitektura* was
devoted to schemes by foreign architects, including Le
Corbusier, Bruno Taut, Frank Lloyd Wright: details of the
contents of each issue are given in *Ex Libris 6*, 1977 (see note
73) cat.243a.

116 A. I. Bezymenskii, *Komsomoliia: stranitsy epopei*, Moscow:
Kommunisticheskii Soiuz molodezhi, 1928.

117 *Vsesoiuznaia Poligraficheskaia Vystavka: putevoditel'*, Moscow
1927 (Nov). The title page carries the information 'Proekt i
detalirovka El' Lisitskogo, tipograficheskoe oformlenie
S. B. Telingatera (Cup.410.e.87).

118 S. I. Kirsanov, *Slovo predostavliaetsia Kirsanovu*, Moscow, izd.
GIZ, 1930 (C.114.m.19).

119 *Sovremennaia arkhitektura*, No.5, 1930 (C.185.bb.2); this issue
includes a discussion of Leonidov's Palace of Culture.

120 V. V. Khlebnikov, *1. Zverinets ... 2. Pis'mo Khlebnikova
3. Vospominaniia o Khlebnikove*, ed. by A. E. Kruchenykh,
Moscow 1930 (Cup.408.i.39); V. V. Khlebnikov, *Neizdannyi
Khlebnikov*: vypusk XIX, *Morskoi bereg*, 1930; vypusk XV,
Rychag chashi, 1930; vypusk XVIII, *1912-1914 gg.*, 1930;
vypusk XVII, *Vila i Leshii; Perun*, 1930. All parts ed. by
A. Kruchenykh, Moscow: Izd. "Gruppy Druzei Khlebnikova"
(C.114.mm.38).

121 V. V. Maiakovskii, *Groznyi smekh: okna Rosta*, ed. by
K. Soliadzhin, Moscow/Leningrad: Gosudarstvennoe

122 *Brigada khudozhnikov*, No.4, 1931, p.23. English transl. by
Peter Nisbet, 'El Lissitzky, Do not separate form from
content!' in his *El Lissitzky 1890-1941*, exhibition catalogue,
Harvard University Art Museums, 1987, pp.61-2. *Industriia
sotsializma: tiazhelaia promyshlennost'*, k VII Vsesoiuznomu
S''ezdu Sovetov, [Moscow]: Izdanie Stroim ("Za
industrializatsiiu") i Izogiza, ed. by B. M. Tal', 1935 (C.191.b.8).
The book includes the note 'Avtor khudozhestvennogo
postroeniia al'boma El' Lisitskii'.

123 F. I. Panferov, *Bruski*, 4 part novel 1931-1937. Vols.1 and 2,
Moscow: Rossiiskaia Assotsiatsiia Proletarskikh Pisatelei
[RAPP], 1931; Vol.3, Moscow 1934; Vol.4, Moscow 1937; vols.3
and 4, Gos. izdat. "Khudozhestvennaia Literatura" (12590.t.1).

124 The decree is translated and discussed in Brown 1953 (see
note 44), pp.200-1 and chapter XI.

125 Elizabeth Valkenier, *Russian Realist Art, The State and Society:
The Peredvizhniki and Their Tradition*, Ann Arbor 1977.

126 Struve 1971 (see note 74), p.249.

127 Fiodor Panferov, *And Then the Harvest*, transl. from Russian
by Stephen Garry, London 1939.

3 Medium and Message: design, technique and content

1 A. E. Kruchenykh, *Ozhirenie roz: o stikhakh Terent'eva i drugikh*
[Tiflis, 1918 or 1919] (C.104.dd.7). Another cover design for this
book is reproduced in *Kirill Zdanevich and Cubo-Futurism*,
Tiflis 1918-1920, exhibition catalogue, Rachel Adler Gallery,
New York 1987 (unpaginated).

2 A. E. Kruchenykh, *Vselenskaia voina*, Petrograd 1916. The date
given in *Knizhnaia letopis'* is 25 Feb.-3 March, well after
Kruchenykh had left for the south according to the
chronology given here in Chapter 2.

3 The scholar Mary Chamot told the author that she had
learned from Rozanova's sister that Ol'ga never married
Kruchenykh, but lived with him as Goncharova did with
Larionov. Rozanova died suddenly in an epidemic in 1918,
having worked with Malevich and the Suprematist group of
artists the year before.

4 Susan Compton, *The World Backwards, Russian Futurist Books
1912-1916*, London, 1978, pp.43, 86, 113-4.

5 V. Kamenskii, A. Kruchenykh, K. Zdanevich, *1918*, Tiflis 1917;
the page with the list of books is reproduced as D.38/v(G) on
p.243 in Rainer Michael Mason, *Moderne. Postmoderne, deux
cas d'école, l'avant-garde russe et hongroise 1916-1925, Giorgio
de Chirico 1924-1934*, Geneva 1988, pp.241-44, where Mason
cites all the arguments for and against Rozanova's
authorship, coming out against it. His argument caused me
to re-attribute the collages to Kruchenykh in my 'Kruchenij
vive!: introducción a los libros de la vanguardia rusa, 1912-
1925', *La Epoca Heroica obra gráfica de las vanguardias rusa y
húngara 1912-1925*, exhibition catalogue, Ivam centre Julio
Gonzales, Valencia 1990, pp.27-35.

6 I. Terent'ev, *Fakt*, Tiflis, 41°, 1919 (C.114.r.5).

7 The poster is reproduced in B. Livshits, *Polutoraglazyi strelets*,
Leningrad: Izdatel'stvo pisatelei v Leningrade, 1933 (X.429/
1069), p.165.

8 I. Terent'ev, *A. Kruchenykh grandiozar'*, [Tiflis 1919] (C.185.a.13).

9 A. E. Kruchenykh, *Lakirovannoe triko*, Tiflis: 41°, 1919
(C.114.m.23).

10 The cover bears the words: 'Carrà futurista: Guerrapittura, futurismo politico, dinamismo plastico, disegni guerreschi, parole in libertà, Edizioni Futuriste di "Poesia", Milan 1915'. It is reproduced in Achille Bonito Oliva, *La parola totale: una tradizione futurista 1909-1986*, exhibition catalogue, Galleria Fonte d'Abisso, Modena 1986, cat.18, p.46.

11 Olga Djordjadze, 'Ilia Zdanevich et le futurisme russe', *Iliazd*, exhibition catalogue, Centre Georges Pompidou, Paris 1978, p.9; Lopatinskii is not identified further: a Boris Lopatinskii was writing exhibition reviews in Moscow in the early 1920s.

12 I. Zdanevich, *Ianko krul' albanskai*, Tiflis 1918 (May). Zdanevich wrote the play in Petrograd where it was performed on 16 December 1916, see Vladimir Markov, *Russian Futurism: A History*, London 1969, pp.351 and 417, n.133.

13 Janecek discusses similarities between Zdanevich's play and Zurich Dada in Gerald Janecek, 'Ilia Zdanevich's "Aslaablic'e" and the transcription of "zaum" in drama', *L'Avanguardia a Tiflis: studi, ricerche, cronache, testimonianze, documenti*, ed. by Luigi Magarotto, Marzio Marzaduri and Giovanna Pagani Cesa, (Quaderni del seminario di iranistica, ural-altaistica e caucasologia; Vol.13) Venice: Universita degli studi di Venezia, 1982, p.36 and p.42, n.8. No visit to Zurich is mentioned in the extensive biography given in *Iliazd* 1978 (see note 11); a copy of the Dada alamanac, *Cabaret Voltaire*, may have reached Petrograd from Zurich in 1916 but this requires research into diplomatic connections and the postal service during the First World War.

14 See Marzio Marzaduri, 'Futurismo Menscevico', *L'Avanguardia a Tiflis*, 1982 (see previous note), p.169.

15 Iliazd (pseud. adopted by Il'ia Zdanevich when he settled in Paris), *aslaab''llch'ia: virtEp f 5 dEistvakh, dEistva 5, lidantIU fAram*, Paris 1923 (C.145.b.15). The reference to Ribemont-Dessaignes is from Marzaduri, as previous note.

16 Pages of copy No.3 of Stepanova's *Gaust chaba* (issued in 1919 in 50 plus 4 numbered copies) are reproduced in *Russische Avantgarde 1910-1930, Sammlung Ludwig, Köln*, ed. by Evelyn Weiss, Munich 1986, pp.162-3; see also *Von der Fläche zum Raum/From Surface to Space: Russland/Russia 1916-24*, Galerie Gmurzynska, Cologne 1974, pp.143-150 and in the same exhibition catalogue, Evgenii Kovtun, 'Varvara Stepanova's Anti-Book', pp.57-63; although the book exhibited on that occasion was the one bought for the Ludwig collection, the photographs reproduced in the catalogue show variations and are not from the same copy.

17 Reproduced in Alexander Lavrentiev, *Varvara Stepanova: a Constructivist Life*, transl. from Russian by Wendy Salmond, ed. by John E. Bowlt, London 1988, pp.19-29.

18 On the next to last page of *Zudesnik* (see note 25 below) is the information: 'Knigi A. Kruchenykh za vremia s 1912 po 1921g vzletelo 97 knig. V 1921g vzleteli: Zamaul' I, II, III & iubileinaia; Tsvetistye tortsy; Miatezh I-IX; Malakholiia v kapote (Anal'naia erotika) 2 izd. i drugie. 1922-ogo g.: Zaum'; Tsotsa (oblozhki A. Rodchenko); Golodniak; Zzudo; Zaumniki: sbornik A. Kruchenykh, V. Khlebnikov, G. Petnikov (oblozhka avto-lino Rodchenko).'

19 Stepanova's exhibition poster, a poster in similar lettering for a debate held on 25.ix.21 and a title page of the catalogue decorated with coloured numbers are reproduced in colour

20 The publication date of *Zaum* is given as 1922 on the back cover of *Zudesnik* (see notes 18 above and 25 below); the cover is reproduced in Selim O. Khan-Magomedov, *Rodchenko the Complete Work*, transl. from Italian by Huw Evans, ed. by Vieri Quillici, London 1986, p.117.

21 A. Kruchenykh, V. Khlebnikov, G. Petnikov, *Zaumniki*, Moscow: EUY, 1922 (C.114.n.37) The book contains an unidentified frontispiece collage, possibly by Rodchenko.

22 A. M. Rodchenko, *Linea*, INKhUK archives. A sketch for the cover of this unpublished pamphlet contains the seeds of Rodchenko's later designs – the two words 'linea' and 'Rodchenko', hand-written in black capitals near the top and bottom of the cover, are linked by a thin diagonal; it is reproduced in Khan-Magomedov 1986 (see note 20), p.293.

23 A. E. Kruchenykh, *Tsotsa*, no further details; fastened into the centre of this book of pages made by hectography and rubber stamping is a printed sheet 'Deklaratsiia zaumnogo iazyka' signed 'A. Kruchenykh, Baku 1921' (C.185.a.30). There is a collaged photograph on the otherwise similar cover for *Tsotsa* reproduced in *Von der Malerei zum Design, Russische konstruktivistische Kunst der Zwanziger Jahre/ From Painting to Design, Russian Constructivist Art of the Twenties*, exhibition catalogue, Galerie Gmurzynska, Cologne 1981, p.219.

24 *Kino-Fot*, No.1, 25-31 August, 1922; No.2, 8-15 September, 1922; No.3, 19-25 September, 1922, No.4, 5-12 October, 1922; No.5, 10 December, 1922, No.6, the final number, came out at the end of January 1923: issues were designed by Gan, Stepanova and Rodchenko.

25 A. E. Kruchenykh, *Zudesnik: zudutnie zudesa* (Kniga 119-aia), Moscow 1922, (C.142.cc.9).

26 A. E. Kruchenykh, *Golodniak*, Moscow, 1922, (C.142.cc.28).

27 A. E. Kruchenykh, *Faktura slova: deklaratsiia*, (MAF: seriia teorii, No.1) Moscow: MAF, 1923 (C.114.m.30); A. E. Kruchenykh, *Sdvigologiia russkogo stikha: trakhtat obizhal'nyi i pouchal'nyi*, (MAF: seriia teorii No.2) 1923 (C.114.m.29); A. E. Kruchenykh, *Apokalipsis v russkoi literature*; *Chort i rechetvortsy*; *Tainye poroki akademikov*; *Slovo kak takovoe*; *Deklaratsii*, Kniga 122-ia, (MAF: seriia teorii, No.3), 1923 (C.114.m.31). MAF is an acronym for Moskovskaia- v Budushchem Mezhdunarodnaia-Assotsiatsiia Futuristov.

28 V. V. Maiakovskii, *Liubliu*, Vtoroe izdanie, (MAF: seriia poetov, No.1) Moscow, Izd. Vkhutemasa, 1922 (C.108.bb.44); N. N. Aseev, *Stal'noi solovei*, vtoroe dopolnennoe i ispravlennoe izdanie, (MAF: seriia poetov No.2) Moscow: Izd. Vkhutemasa, 1922 (C.108.bb.44); V. V. Maiakovskii, *Maiakovskii izdevaetsia: pervaia knizhitsa satiry*, 2.izd., (MAF: seriia poetov No.3), Moscow: Izd. Vkhutemasa, 1922 (C.136.b.32).

29 B. L. Pasternak, A. E. Kruchenykh, S. M. Tret'iakov, D. Burliuk, and others, *Zhiv Kruchenykh!* Moscow: Izdanie Vserossiiskogo soiuza poetov, [1925] (C.114.m.26).

30 Iurii Libedinskii remembered Kruchenykh at a meeting held early in 1923; cited in English in Wiktor Woroszylski, *The Life of Mayakovsky*, transl. from Polish by Boleslaw Taborski, London 1972, p.323.

31 A. E. Kruchenykh, *Zaumnyi iazyk u Seifullinoi, Vs. Ivanova, Leonova, Babelia, I. Sel'vinskogo, A. Veselogo i dr.* Kniga 127-ia; Moscow: Izdanie Vserossiiskogo soiuza poetov, 1925 (C.114.m.25).

32 V. V. Maiakovskii, *Maiakovskii ulybaetsia, Maiakovskii smeetsia, Maiakovskii izdevaetsia*, Moscow/Petersburg: Krug, 1923 (Cup.408.d.25).

33 A. E. Kruchenykh, with Aliagrov (pseudonym of Roman Iakobson), *Iazyk Lenina: odinnadtsat' priemov Leninskoi rechi*, Moscow: Izdanie Vserossiiskogo soiuza poetov, 1925 (C.136.b.30).

34 *Staatliches Bauhaus in Weimar 1919-1923*, Weimar, Bauhaus verlag, 1923; the cover is reproduced in *Kandinsky: Russian and Bauhaus Years 1915-1933*, exhibition catalogue, The Solomon R. Guggenheim Museum, New York 1983, p.346. The library of *VKhUTEMAS* included all the Bauhaus books, see Szymon Bojko, *New Graphic Design in Revolutionary Russia*, transl. from Polish by Robert Strybel and Lech Zembrzuski, London 1972, p.22.

35 *Let: sbornik stikhov*, ed. by N. N. Aseev, Moscow: Krasnaia nov'', 1923. The cover is entitled '*Let: avio stikhi*' (Cup.408.g.43).

36 An advertisement for Dobrolet is reproduced in colour in *Soviet Commercial Design of the Twenties*, ed. by Mikhail Anikst, transl. by Catherine Cooke, London 1987, plate 139, p.83.

37 The British Library has a microfilm of Aleksei Gan, *Konstruktivizm*, Tver', Tver'skoe izdatel'stvo, 1922 (Mic.A.7177). The cover is reproduced in *The Tradition of Constructivism*, ed. by Stephen Bann, New York 1974, opp. p.35; the design has been described as by Gan himself, but Khan-Magomedov establishes it as by Rodchenko, in Khan-Magomedov 1986 (see note 20), p.131, where Rodchenko's first design for the cover is reproduced on p.133.

38 Film titles and captions by Rodchenko are reproduced in *From Painting to Design* 1981 (see note 23), pp. 75, 77-81.

39 'Konstruktivisti', *LEF* No.1, 1923, p.251, unsigned; cited in English in Vlada Petrić, *Constructivism in Film: 'The Man with a Movie Camera', A Cinematic Analysis*, Cambridge 1987, p.12.

40 Gan's *Konstruktivizm* is partially translated in Bann 1074 (acc note 37), pp.33-42.

41 S. P. Bobrov, *Vosstanie mizantropov*, Moscow: Tsentrifuga, 1922 (Cup.408.d.35).

42 Joseph Freeman, 'The Soviet Cinema' in Joseph Freeman, Joshua Kunitz, Louis Lozowick, *Voices of October: Art and Literature in Soviet Russia*, New York 1930, p.260.

43 *Kino-fot*, No.3, 8-15 September, 1922, pp.11,12. 'Detektiv' is reproduced in A. N. Lavrent'ev, *A. M. Rodchenko, V. F. Stepanova*, (Mastera sovetskogo knizhnogo iskusstva), Moscow 1989, fig.62.

44 V. V. Maiakovskii, *Pro eto*, Moscow/Petrograd: Izdatel'stvo LEF; Gosizdat, 1923 (August) (C.131.k.12).

45 Oscar Wilde, *The Ballad of Reading Gaol*, London 1898. A Russian translation by Kornei Chukovskii had recently been published, according to Robert C. Williams, *Artists in Revolution: Portraits of the Russian Avant-garde 1905-1925*, London 1978, p.145.

46 The photographers are named as Wasserman, Kapustshanskii and Sterenberg on the title page of *Pro eto*.

47 *Zakovannaia filmoi*, Neptune, director N. Turkin, scenario by Maiakovskii, who acted with Lili Brik, Margarita Kibalchich and A. Rebikova; the film was released in June 1918; see Jay Leyda, *Kino. A History of Russian and Soviet Film*, London 1960, p.424.

48 Cited without source in Woroszylski 1972 (see note 30), p.320.

49 Maiakovskii's films are discussed in Boleslav Rostotsky, 'Mayakovsky and the cinema', one of a collection of essays by various authors, entitled *Vladimir Mayakovsky: Innovator*, transl. from Russian by Alex Miller, Moscow 1976, pp.120-36.

50 Jim Dollar (pseudonym for Marietta Sergeevna Shaginian), *Mess Mend ili IAnki v Petrograde: roman*, Moscow/Petrograd, Gosizdat, 1924 (C.185.a.32). All the covers are reproduced in colour in Claude Leclanche-Boulé, *Typographies et photomontages constructivistes en U.R.S.S.*, Paris 1985, fig.112, p.72-3.

51 *Vestnik truda: ezhemesiachnyi organ Vserossiiskogo Tsentral'nogo Soveta Professional'nykh Soiuzov*, Moscow: Izdatel. VTSPS, No.1, 1925 (PP.1423.phk).

52 Iu. N. Libedinskii, *Zavtra*, Moscow/Leningrad: Molodaia gvardiia, 1924 (12840.k.16)

53 Il'ia Lin, *Deti i Lenin*, Moscow: Molodaia gvardiia, 1924; cover and two illustrations reproduced in Gail Harrison Roman, *Ex Libris 6: Constructivism and Futurism: Russian and Other*, New York 1977, cat.155.

54 A. N. Lavrentiev, 'Photographie, poésie et réalité', *Paris-Moscou*, exhibition catalogue, Musée nationale d'art moderne, Centre Georges Pompidou, Paris 1978, p.510, author's translation.

55 The unsigned article is partially translated by Michael Skinner in Dawn Ades, *Photomontage*, revised and enlarged edition, London 1986, p.72. Citroën's *Metropolis* is reproduced on p.98.

56 Photographs of Popova's montage and the surviving panel are reproduced in *Russian Avant-Garde Art: The George Costakis Collection*, ed. by A. Z. Rudenstine, New York and London 1981, pp.402 and 403, Cats. 887, 889.

57 V. V. Maiakovskii, *Razgovor s fininspektorom o poezii*, Tiflis: Zakkniga, 1926 (C.136.b.34).

58 Last lines of *Razgovor* (see previous note) transl. by Herbert Marshall, *Mayakovsky*, New York 1965: 'A Conversation with the Inspector of Taxes about Poetry', pp.351-59; this citation from p.359.

59 V. V. Maiakovskii, *Sifilis*, Tiflis: Zakkniga, [1926] (C.114.mm.12).

60 I. G. Erenburg, *Materializatsiia fantastiki*, (Kino-pechat', No.126) Moscow/Leningrad: Kinopechat', 1927 (C.136.b.35).

61 Both *Sifilis* and *Razgovor* were published in Tiflis by Zakkniga (see notes 57 and 59 above).

62 I. Sel'vinskii, *Zapiski poeta*, Moscow/Leningrad: Gikhl, 1928, (Cup.410.f.69).

63 *391*, No.XII, March 1920.

64 Gail Weber, 'Constructivism and Soviet Literature', *Soviet Union* 3, part 2, 1976, p.299.

65 *Arkhitektura: raboty arkhitekturnogo fakul'teta Vkhutemasa, 1920-1927*, Moscow: Izdanie Vkhutemasa, 1927 (Sept.) (C.190.aaa.25).

66 Lissitzky's photograph, entitled 'The Constructor', is reproduced in Sophie Lissitzky-Küppers, *El Lissitzky, Life, Letters, Texts*, transl. from German by Helen Aldwinckle and Mary Whittall, London 1980, fig.118. Lissitzky used the photograph of his hand as though it were a picture, hanging it on the wall of his First Exhibition Room in Dresden in 1926; it is shown in a photograph in Lissitzky-Küppers, fig.192.

67 Lissitzky used the technique for his advertisments for

Pelikan ink made in 1924. For a reproduction of a photogram by Man Ray with a description of the technique see *Merz*, Vol.2, no.8-9, April-July, 1924, Hanover; this issue was edited by Lissitzky as well as Kurt Schwitters.

68 *Sovetskoe foto*, No.10, 15 May 1929, p.311; transl. by Peter Nisbet in *El Lissitzky 1890-1941, Architect, Painter, Photographer, Typographer*, exhibition catalogue, Municipal Van Abbemuseum, Eindhoven 1990, p.70.

69 El Lissitzky, article in *Ringen*, No.10, (1922) (Warsaw), pp.32-4, transl. from the Yiddish as 'The conquest of Art', by Michael Steinlauf in Peter Nisbet, *El Lissitzky (1890-1941)*, exhibition catalogue, Busch-Reisinger Museum, Harvard University 1987, pp.59-61.

70 El Lissitzky, *Russland, die Rekonstruktion der Architektur in der Sowjetunion*, (Neues Bauen in der Welt, Vol.I), Vienna 1930 (Cup.410.g.7).

71 V.V. Maiakovskii, *Dlia golosa*, Berlin: Gosudarstvennoe izdatel'stvo, 1923 (C.114.mm.33). Facsimile reprint, Cologne and New York, 1973.

72 El Lissitzky, *Die plastische Gestaltung der elektro-mechanischen Schau, Sieg über die Sonne, als Oper gedichtet von A. Krutschonjch, Moskau 1913*; ten lithographs in 75 numbered copies with title page and portolio cover, Hanover 1923; six lithographs are reproduced in colour in Lissitzky-Küppers 1980 (see note 66), plates 55, 58-62. A new production of the Futurist opera, *Pobeda nad solntsem*, was planned by Malevich at the Vitebsk Art School in 1920 while Lissitzky was teaching there.

73 El Lissitzky's article is quoted without further source as 'Typographical facts', in Lissitzky-Küppers 1980 (see note 66) where it is given as the caption to plates 95-108; the decorated page openings from *Dlia golosa* are reproduced in colour on the same pages.

74 Boris Pil'niak, *Povest' Peterburgskaia*, Moscow/Berlin: Gelikon, 1922 (012590.c.21).

75 *Epopeia: literaturnyi ezhemesiachnik*, ed. by Andrei Belyi, No.1, April 1922; No.2, September 1922; No.3, January 1923 (though December 1922 on cover), Moscow/Berlin: Gelikon (PP.4842.dcb). Lissitzky's covers have elements coloured yellow on No.1, green, on No.2, grey on No.3. The contents of the journal are described in *Ex Libris 6*, 1977 (see note 53), cat.54.

76 A.A. Blok, *Dvenadtsat'*, Berlin: Neva, [1922] (11585.l.35).

77 V.V. Maiakovskii, *Chelovek; Veshch'*, [Moscow]: Izd. ASIS, [1918] (C.114.mm.11).

78 Ivanov-Razumnik (pseud. of Razumnik Vasil'evich Ivanov) *Vladimir Maiakovskii 'Misteriia' ili 'Buff'*, Berlin: Skify, 1922 (Cup.410.f.72).

79 See Chapter 2, note 66, for listing of these periodicals.

80 For example, *Vsesoiuznaia Poligraficheskaia Vystavka: putevoditel'*, Moscow 1927 (Cup.410.e.87); Lissitzky also designed Soviet exhibitions abroad, for example, *Führer durch die Ausstellung der Union der Sozialistischen Sowjet-Republiken auf der Internatsionalen Pelzfach-Ausstellung 1930*, Leipzig, 1930 (Cup.410.g.8).

81 S.M. Tret'iakov, *Rechevik: stikhi*, Moscow/Leningrad: Gosudarstvennoe izdatel'stvo, 1929 (011586.f.92). Back and front covers are reproduced in Lavrent'ev 1989 (see note 43), fig.50.

4 Theatre: a revolution in design

1 Joseph Gregor and René Fülöp-Miller, *The Russian Theatre*, transl. by Paul England, London 1930 (11795.tt.15). A recent study by Konstantin Rudnitsky, *Russian and Soviet Theatre: Tradition and the Avant-Garde*, transl. from Russian by Roxane Permar, ed. by Dr. Lesley Milne, London 1988, provides an indispensable view from a modern perspective.

2 N.N. Evreinov, *Teatral'nye novatsii*, Petrograd: Tret'ia strazha, 1922 (011840.m.64).

3 (Carlo) Count Gozzi, *Printsessa Turandot*, Moscow/Petrograd: Gosudarstvennoe izdatel'stvo, [1923] (11795.tt.14).

4 Rudnitsky 1988 (see note 1) gives a description of the production and reproduces photographs.

5 *Masterstvo teatra: vremennik Kamernogo teatra*, No.1, Dec. 1922, [Moscow]: Izdatels'tvo [sic] Russkogo teatral'nogo obshchestva, 1922 (C.191.b.3).

6 Abram M. Efros, *Kamernyi teatr i ego khudozhniki 1914-1934*, Moscow: Izdanie Vserossiiskogo teatral'nogo obshchestva, 1934 (11795.tt.44).

7 Ia.V. Apushkin, *Kamernyi teatr*, Moscow/Leningrad: Kinopechat', 1927 (X.989/75870).

8 A.Ia. Tairov, *Zapiski rezhissera*, Moscow: Izd. Kamernogo teatra, 1921 (December) (C.114.l.4). Illustrations and cover reproduced in *A.Ia. Tairov, Zapiski rezhissera: stat'i, besedy, rechi, pis'ma*, ed. by P. Markov, Moscow: Vserossiiskoe teatral'noe obshchestvo, 1970, p.71 ff. English transl. by William Kuhlke, *Notes of a Director by A. Tairov* (Books of the Theater No.7), Miami 1969.

9 Ia. Tugendkhol'd, *Aleksandra Ekster kak zhivopisets i khudozhnik stseny*, Berlin, 1922 (7862.ppp.17). English translation: Ia. Tugendhold, *Alexandra Exter*, transl. by Count Petrovsky-Petrovo-Solovovo, Berlin: Saria 1922. French translation: Jacques Tugendhold, *Alexandra Exter*, traduit du manuscrit russe, Saria 1922 (7868.f.13).

10 The technique of using a plain backcloth coloured by lighting was developed by Alexander von Saltzman, for Adophe Appia at the Jacques-Dalcroze theatre at Hellerau, Switzerland; on a visit to Russia, Saltzman gave Tairov exclusive rights to his system in Russia for three years, see Oliver M. Sayler, *The Russian Theatre under the Revolution*, Boston, 1920, p.149.

11 Andrei Nakov reproduced the cover using Roman letters, for his *Alexandra Exter*, exhibition catalogue, Galerie Jean Chauvelin, Paris 1972.

12 German translation, first published in 1923 with publication details similar to the British Library copy: A.Ia. Tairov, *Das entfesselte Theater. Aufzeichnungen eines Regisseurs* (second edition) authorized transl. from the Russian, Potsdam 1927 (11795.dd.54).

13 Aleksandr Gorin, *Kto, chto, kogda v Moskovskom Kamernom teatre*, [Moscow, 1924?] (Cup.1264.gg.23).

14 See Selim O. Khan-Magomedov, *Pioneers of Soviet Architecture, The Search for New Solutions in the 1920s and 1930s*, transl. from Russian by Alexander Lieven, ed. by Catherine Cooke, London 1987, pp.153-4.

15 Models and setting are reproduced in Khan-Magomedov 1987 (see previous note): Vesnin's model p.175, figs.466-7; Popova's set, p.174, fig.463.

16 Sketch and models are reproduced in Khan-Magomedov 1987 (see note 14), p.173, figs.460-62.

17 The outstanding production in this vein had been of Aleksandr Blok's *Balaganchik* in 1914; for a description see Edward Braun, *The Theatre of Meyerhold, Revolution on the Modern Stage*, London 1979, pp.127-30.

18 *Pechat' i revoliutsiia*, No.1, 1922, pp.305-9; English transl. in Edward Braun, *Meyerhold on Theatre*, London 1969, p.201. Braun also translates a report on a lecture on biomechanics by Meyerhold (pp.197-200). A full description of biomechanics is given in Rudnitsky 1988 (see note 1), pp.93-4.

19 Ia. Brukson, *Teatr Meierkhol'da*, Leningrad/Moscow: Kniga, 1925 (X.908/6098).

20 *LEF*, No.4, 1924, p.43. This number is not in the British Library collection.

21 There is a photograph showing an out-of-doors production in Braun 1969 (see note 18), following p.184.

22 V. V. Maiakovskii, *Misteriia-Buff*, Petrograd: Svoboda, 1918 (C.135.g.23).

23 The poster for *Mystery-Bouffe* is reproduced in Braun 1979 (see note 17), p.149, where there is a full description of the production, pp.148-52.

24 A. E. Kruchenykh, *Pobeda nad solntsem: opera*, music by M. Matiushin, St Petersburg: EUY, 1913 (C.114.mm.9). There is a set design by K. Malevich on the cover, reproduced in Susan Compton, *The World Backwards: Russian Futurist Books, 1912-1916*, London 1978, p.59 and see pp.52-61 for a description of the production.

25 V. V. Maiakovskii, *Misteriia-Buff*, vtoroe izdanie, Moscow; Petrograd [1922] (11758.h.46). also V. Maiakovskii, *Misteriia-Buff*, vtoraia redaktsiia k tret'emu izdaniiu, (*Vestnik teatra*, No.90/91) Moscow: Teatral'nyi otdel Glavpolit-prosveta, [1922] (11758.m.29). English translation described as '1921 revised version' in George R. Noyes, *Masterpieces of the Russian Drama*, New York and London 1933.

26 V. V. Khlebnikov, *Zangezi*, Moscow [1922] (August) (C.114.n.42). See *Tatlin*, ed. by Larissa Zhadova, London, 1988, p.397. English transl. of 'Plane 9' (one of the twenty sections) by Gary Kern in *The Ardis Anthology of Russian Futurism*, ed. by Ellendea Proffer and Carl Proffer, Ann Arbor 1980, pp.24-6. Miturich had married Khlebnikov's sister and when the poet died of malnutrition and exhaustion on June 28, 1922 in the village of Santalov, he had drawn sketches of his death bed reproduced in E. Zhukova, *Petr Vasil'evich Miturich 1887-1956. K 90-letiiu so dnia rozhdeniia*, State Tret'iakov Gallery, Moscow 1978, cat.88 (unpaginated) Two drawings were reproduced in *Russkoe Iskusstvo*, No.2/3, 1923, opp.p.99 (P.P.1931.pmh).

27 Cited by Kern in *Ardis Anthology* 1980 (see previous note) p.32.

28 Described as 'prostranstvennaia grafika', none has survived but photographs are published in Zhukova 1978 (see note 26); the catalogue is unpaginated.

29 Examples are reproduced in colour in *Art into Life: Russian Constructivism 1914-1932*, exhibition catalogue, [Henry Art Gallery of the University of Washington, Seattle, Walker Art Center, Minneapolis], New York 1990, p.41.

30 For discussion of Tatlin's work as a theatre designer see Flora Iakovlevna Surkina, 'Tatlin's theatre' in Zhadova ed. 1980 (see note 26).

31 *Russkoe iskusstvo*, No.1, 1923, opp. p.20 (P.P.1931.pmh).

32 Iu. Tynianov, introduction to Velimir Khlebnikov, *Sobranie Sochinenii*, Leningrad: 1928, translated in *The Futurists, the Formalists, and the Marxist Critique*, ed. and introduction by Christopher Pike, transl. by Christopher Pike and Joe Andrew, London 1979, p.148.

33 Andrei Globa, *Famar': tragediia*, Moscow: Gosudarstvennoe izdatel'stvo [1923] (X.900/20598).

34 Vladimir Favorskii won the Grand Prix for his wood engravings at the international exhibition of decorative arts in Paris in 1925. The exhibition 'Wladimir Favorsky 50 years of his Graphic Art 1912-1961' was held in London in 1962 at the Grosvenor Gallery; see Yuri Molok, *Vladimir Favorsky*, Moscow 1967 (English text). Favorsky's teaching activities are cited by Christina Lodder, *Russian Constructivism*, London 1983, p.242.

35 Abram Efros, article in *Russkoe iskusstvo*, No.1, 1923, English transl. as 'Favorsky and modern xylography', in Molok 1967 (see previous note), pp.23-7.

36 A. Terek (pseud. of Ol'ga Forsh) *Ravvi: p'esa v trekh deistviiakh*, Berlin: Skify, 1922 (11758.r.17). A list of publications inside back cover includes the information about a Moscow edition, published by Krug, with a cover by L'ev Bruni.

37 *Veshch'/Gegenstand/Objet: révue internationale de l'art moderne*, No.1/2, 1922, Berlin: Skythen, (Cup.408.g.25).

38 V. V. Maiakovskii, *Klop: feericheskaia komediia, deviat' kartin*, Moscow/Leningrad: Gosudarstvennoe izdatel'stvo, 1929 (August) (C.133.b.18). English translation by Max Hayward in Michael V. Glenny, *Three Soviet Plays*, Penguin Plays No. PL62, Harmondsworth 1966.

39 *Vsesoiuznaia Poligraficheskaia Vystavka: putevoditel'* Moscow: Izdanie K-ta Vsesoiuznoi Poligraficheskoi Vystavki, 1927 (November) (Cup.410.e.87).

40 Although the cover is unsigned and no name of a designer is given inside the book, it is attributed to Rodchenko in Selim O. Khan-Magomedov, *Rodchenko, The Complete Work*, transl. from Italian by Huw Evans, ed. by Vieri Quillici, London 1986, p.139.

41 V. V. Maiakovskii, *Bania: drama v 6-ti deistviiakh s tsirkom i feierverkom*, Moscow/Leningrad: Gosudarstvennoe izdatel'stvo, 1930 (011388.d.10). English transl. in Andrew T. MacAndrew, *20th Century Russian Drama*, New York 1963 and Guy Daniels, *The Complete Plays of V. Mayakovsky*, transl. by Guy Daniels, New York 1968.

42 See Valentin Pluchek, 'The New Drama', in a collection of essays by various authors, entitled, *Vladimir Mayakovsky: Innovator*, transl. from Russian by Alex Miller, Moscow 1976, pp.96-7.

43 Boleslav Rostotsky, 'Mayakovsky and the Cinema' points out that filmscripts by Maiakovskii (which he translates as 'Forget the Fireside' and 'History of a Revolver') were written immediately before *The Bed Bug* and both contributed to the plot; Rostotsky's article is in *Vladimir Mayakovsky: Innovator* 1976 (see previous note), p.135.

44 'Kukryniksy' was the name adopted by three young artists, Mikhail Kupriianov, Porfirii Krylov, Nikolai Sokolov, who also worked as cartoonists; production photographs and designs are reproduced in Rudnitsky 1988 (see note 1), pp.256-9.

45 S. M. Tret'iakov, *Slyshish', Moskva?! Agit-gin'ol' v 4-kh deistviiakh*, (Repertuar Proletkul'ta), Moscow: Vserossiiskii proletkul't, 1924 (X.902/3151).

46 The production is described more fully in Rudnitsky 1988 (see note 1), p.96.

47 A.N.Afinogenov, *Na perelome (v riady): drama v 4 deistviiakh i v 8 kartinakh*, (Repetuar teatra Proletkul'ta), Moscow: Moskovskoe teatral'noe izdatel'stvo, 1927 (C.191.a.17).

48 A.N.Afinogenov, *Na perelome* is listed among books illustrated by the artist in *Kirill Zdanevich and Cubo-Futurism: Tiflis 1918-1920*, exhibition catalogue, Rachel Adler Gallery, New York 1987, unpaginated.

49 V.V.Maiakovskii, *Chto ne stranitsa – to slon, to l'vitsa*, [Tiflis] Zakkniga, 1928; an opening of the book is reproduced as cat.88, in *Kirill Zdanevich* 1987 (see previous note).

V.V.Khlebnikov, *1. Zverinets*, ed. by A.Kruchenykh, Moscow: Izdanie 'Gruppy druzei Khlebnikova', 1930 (Cup.408.i.39).

50 Information on Aleksandr Nikolaevich Afinogenov (1904-41) is given in Gleb Struve, *Russian Literature under Lenin and Stalin 1917-1953*, Oklahoma 1971, pp.305-6; his ideas are discussed by Rudnitsky 1988 (see note 1), pp.208 and 265.

51 *LEF*, No.1, 1924, pp.23-33.

52 A description of the productions is given in Rudnitsky 1988 (see note 1), pp.197-8 with a production photograph on p.234.

53 Braun 1969 (see note 18), p.233.

54 *Novyi LEF*, No.3, 1927, pp.3-11.(This issue is not in the British Library holding.)

55 A photograph of Lissitzky's model from the Bakhrushin Museum, Moscow, is reproduced in Braun 1969 (see note 18), opp. p.257.

56 Platon Kerzhentsev, article in *Pravda*, 17 Dec. 1937, English translation as 'An Alien Theatre', in Braun 1979 (see note 17), pp.264-5.

57 *Pikovaia dama: opera v 4 deistviiakh: muzyka P.I.Chaikovskogo: sbornik statei i materialov k postanovke opery Pikovaia dama narodnym artistom Respubliki Vs.E.Meierkhol'dom v Gosudarstvennom akademicheskom malom opernom teatre*, ed. by A.Krolenko, Leningrad: Gosudarstvennyi akademicheskii Malyi opernyi teatr, 1935 (C.191.b.5). Meyerhold's essay, 'Pushkin i Chaikovskii', pp.5-11 is transl. in Braun 1969 (see note 18), pp.278-89.

58 A description of the production and the alteration of the libretto is given in Braun 1979 (see note 17), pp.256-9.

59 A.S.Griboedov, *Gore ot uma v postanovke Moskovskogo Khudozhestvennogo Teatra*, [by Vladimir Nemirovich-Danchenko], Moscow/Petrograd: Gos.iz/Edition de l'état, 1923 (11758.m.22).

60 Stanislavskii died on 7 August 1938, reputedly having said 'Take care of Meyerhold; he is my sole heir in the theatre – here or anywhere else'; Meyerhold became artistic director of Stanislavskii's Opera Studio in October 1938 but was arrested in June 1939, the day after making a speech at the All-Union Conference of Stage Directors; he is believed to have been shot on 2 February 1940 in a Moscow prison, Braun 1969 (see note 18) pp.251-2.

5 Utopian Ideas in Art and Architecture

1 See Selim O.Khan-Magomedov, *Pioneers of Soviet Architecture: The Search for New Solutions in the 1920s and 1930s*, ed. by Catherine Cooke, transl. from Russian by Alexander Lieven, London 1987, chapter 1.

2 *Novyi mir*, No.9, 1966, p.239, English transl. in Khan-Magomedov 1987 (see previous note), p.24.

3 See Selim O.Khan-Magomedov, *Rodchenko the Complete Works*, transl. from Italian by Huw Evans, ed. by Vieri Quilici, London 1986, p.54.

4 Antonio Sant'Elia's manifesto of Futurist architecture of 11 July 1914 (amplified from catalogue intro. 'Nuove tendenze, Milan 1914' was published in *Lacerba*, 1 August 1914; transl. by Caroline Tisdall in *Futurist Manifestos*, ed. by Umbro Apollonio, London 1973, pp.160-172. Connections between Russian and Italian Futurists had been cemented after the visit of Filippo Marinetti to Russia in January 1914, when Nikolai Kul'bin, Rozanova and Ekster had sent work to a Futurist exhibition in Rome in April; Russian translations of Futurist manifestos were published later in 1914.

5 Designs by G.Mapu, Krinskii and Ladovskii are reproduced in Khan-Magomedov 1987 (see note 1), plates 213-8, pp.85-6; plates 890-2 and 893-4, p.349. Khan-Magomedov discusses Housing Communes as well as these designs on pp.342-3.

6 Both Chagall and Lissitzky illustrated many books which, because they are written in Yiddish, fall outside the scope of this study. A full discussion is found in *Tradition and Revolution, The Jewish Renaissance in Russian Avant-Garde Art 1912-1928*, ed. by Ruth Apter-Gabriel, exhibition catalogue, The Israel Museum, Jerusalem 1987.

7 A.Efros and Ia.Tugₑndkhol'd, *Iskusstvo Marka Shagala*, Moscow: Gelikon, 1918 (C.114.n.30).

8 For a fuller account of Chagall in Russia see Susan Compton, 'The Russian Background', *Chagall*, exhibition catalogue, Royal Academy of Arts, London and Philadelphia Museum of Art, 1985, pp.30-45.

9 K.S.Malevich, *O novykh sistemakh v iskusstve*, Vitebsk, 1919 (C.114.n.46, Mic.A.7632). The lithographed cover by El Lissitzky is reproduced in Susan Compton, *The World Backwards: Russian Futurist Books 1912-16*, London 1978, fig.81, p.113.

10 K.S.Malevich, *Ot Sezanna do suprematizma: kriticheskii ocherk*, [Moscow]: Izdanie Otdela Izobrazitel'nykh Iskusstv Narkomprosa, [1920] (C.114.m.34).

11 See V.Rakitin, 'UNOVIS', *Building in the USSR 1917-1932*, ed. by O.A.Shvidkovskii, London 1971, pp.26-34.

12 For example, *S''ezd komitetov derevenskoi bednoty*, Severnaia oblast' (a prospectus for the Congress of Committees on Peasant Poverty of 1919) has a colour lithograph on the front cover designed by Malevich; it was also issued as a poster. Reproduced in Evgenii Kovtun, 'The Beginning of Suprematism', *Von der Fläche zum Raum/From Surface to Space: Russland/Russia 1916-24*, exhibition catalogue, Galerie Gmurzynska, Cologne 1974, p.47.

13 K.S.Malevich, *K voprosu izobrazitel'nogo iskusstva*, Smolensk: Gosudarstvennoe izdatel'stvo, 1921 (C.185.b.13).

14 K.S.Malevich, *Bog ne skinut: iskusstvo, tserkov', fabrika*, Vitebsk 1922 (C.114.n.33).

15 *K.S.Malevich, Suprematizm: 34 risunki*, facsimile reprint with transl. by Alexander Lieven (from Larissa Zhadova, *Malevich*, London 1982), packaged with Patricia Railing, *On Suprematism 34 Drawings, A Little Handbook of Suprematism*, Artists Bookworks, Forest Row 1990.

16 N.N.Punin, *Pervyi tsikl lektsii, chitannykh na kratkosrochnykh*

kursakh dlia uchitelei risovaniia: sovremennoe iskusstvo,
Petrograd, 1920 (C.114.mm.34).

17 Chagall's etchings for Gogol's *Les Ames Mortes*, fables by
La Fontaine and the Bible, all commissioned by Ambroise
Vollard, are discussed and reproduced in Susan Compton,
Marc Chagall, My Life, My Dream: Berlin and Paris 1922-1940,
Munich 1990.

18 *V. V. Kandinskii: tekst khudozhnika (Stupeni): 25 reproduktsii s
kartin 1902-1917 gg, 4 vin'etki,* Moscow: Izdanie Otdela
Izobrazitel'nykh Iskusstv Narodnogo Komissariata po
Prosveshcheniiu, 1918 (C.104.i.16).

19 V. V. Kandinskii, 'Rückblicke', *Kandinsky 1901-1913*, Berlin, Der
Sturm, (1913). English transl. by Mrs Robert Herbert, in
Modern Artists on Art: Ten Unabridged Essays, ed. by Robert
L. Herbert, New Jersey, Englewood Cliffs, 1964, pp.19-44.

20 V. Kandinskii, 'O stsenicheskoi kompozitsii', *Izobrazitel'noe
iskusstvo*, No.1, 1919, Petersburg, pp.39-49 (L.R.416.tt.10).

21 V. Kandinskii, 'O tochke', *Iskusstvo: Vestnik Otdela
Izobrazitel'nykh Iskusstv Narodnogo Komissariata po
Prosveshcheniiu,* No.3, 1919, Moscow, pp.2-3; V. Kandinskii, 'O
linea', *Iskusstvo: Vestnik Otdela IZO NKP,* No.4, 22 Feb. 1919.
The first page of this number with Kandinskii's vignette/
heading is reproduced in *The Life of Vasilii Kandinsky [sic] in
Russian Art, A Study of 'On the Spiritual in Art',* ed. by John
Bowlt and Rose-Carol Washton Long, transl. from Russian by
John Bowlt, Newtonville, Mass. 1980, p.138; bibliographic
material is given on p.40, n.114.

22 Khan-Magomedov 1986 (see note 3), p.58.

23 A. M. Rodchenko, 'O linea', mss. in INKhUK archives, transl.
in Khan-Magomedov 1986 (see note 3), pp.292-4; Rodchenko's
sketch for the cover is reproduced on p.293.

24 The text of Kandinskii's plan is published in I. Matsa and
others, *Sovetskoe iskusstvo za 15 let*, Moscow/Leningrad: 1933,
pp.126-39.

25 Münsterburg was a prolific writer: originally from
Heidelberg he became a Professor at Harvard, where he was
in charge of a psychotechnical laboratory: he published
many of his books in German as well as English versions
(not translations) See his *Psychology and Industrial Efficiency*,
London 1913, which, he writes, corresponds to his *Psychologie
und Wirtschaftsleben: Ein Beitrag zur angewandten
Experimental-Psychologie,* Leipzig; it is not clear whether the
German book was published in 1912 or 1913.

26 Anatole Kopp, *Constructivist Architecture in the USSR*, transl.
from French by Sheila de Vallée, London and New York 1985,
p.136. Ladovskii's equipment included machines for testing
the angle of vision and the spatial properties of form; some
are reproduced by Khan-Magomedov 1987 (see note 1), plates
378-83, p.136.

27 Aleksei Gan, *Konstruktivizm*, Tver' 1922, p.53, (Mic.A.7177)
transl. from Catherine Cooke, '"Form is a function X": the
development of the constructivist architect's design method',
Russian Avant-Garde Art and Architecture, ed. by Catherine
Cooke, (Architectural Design Profile, Vol.53, 516), London and
New York 1983, p.37.

28 O. Brik, and others, *Iskusstvo v proizvodstve: sborniki
Khudozhestvenno-Proizvodstvennogo Soveta Otdela
Izobrazitel'nykh Iskusstv Narkomprosa,* Vol.I, Moscow 1921
(Cup.410.d.80).

29 English transl. in D. G. B. Piper, *V. A. Kaverin: A Soviet Writer's
Response to the Problem of Commitment,* (Duquesne Studies,
Philological Series), Duquesne 1971, p.43.

30 *Veshch'/Gegenstand/Objet: révue internationale de l'art
moderne,* ed. by El Lissitzky and Il'ia Erenburg, Berlin:
Skythen, 1922, No.1-2, p.3 (Cup.408.g.25). English transl. in
Piper 1971 (see previous note), pp.39-40.

31 See, for example, Lavinskii's cover for O. Brik's *Ne
poputchitsa*, 26, p.56 above.

32 Lissitzky used this nomenclature on the page opposite the
title page in V. V. Maiakovskii, *Dlia golosa* (C.114.mm.33). His
role in disseminating architectural ideas is discussed by
Khan-Magomedov 1987, (see note 1), pp.142, 149.

33 N. Punin, article in *Iskusstvo kommuny*, 9 March, 1919,
Petrograd, pp.2-3, English transl., 'On the Tower', in *Tatlin*,
exhibition catalogue, Moderna Museet, Stockholm, 1968,
pp.56-7.

34 V. Shklovskii, article in *Zhizn' iskusstva*, Nos. 650-52, Jan. 5-9,
1921, p.1, cited in English in *Tatlin* 1968 (as previous note),
p.59.

35 M. Ia. Ginzburg, *Ritm v arkhitekture*, Moscow 1923,
(X.421/22845).

36 M. Ia. Ginzburg, *Stil' i epokha*, Moscow: Gosizdat, 1924
(X.421/22844); English transl. and intro. by Anatole
Senkevitch Jr, *Style and Epoch: Problems of Modern
Architecture,* Cambridge Mass. and London 1982.

37 In the English translation (see previous note) these
photographs are designed into the text in a pseudo-
Constructivist way which gives a somewhat false idea of the
original.

38 English transl. from Senkevitch 1982 (see note 36), p.86.

39 *SA, Sovremennaia Arkhitektura*, Moscow: Gosizdat, 1926-30 ed.
by M. Ginzburg and A. Vesnin. British Library holdings: 1926,
Nos.1-6; 1927, Nos.1-3; 1928, Nos.3, 5; 1929, Nos.1-6; 1930,
Nos.1-6 (C.185.bb.2).

40 *SA*, No.4, 1929 was the first issue designed by Stepanova; the
design of No.5, 1930 is credited to Telingater, and No.3, 1930
can be attributed to him on stylistic grounds.

41 *ASNOVA: Izvestiia Assotsiatsii novykh arkhitektorov/
Mitteilungen der Assotation Neuer Architekten/Revue de
l'Assotation [sic] d'architectes contemporaines,* ed. by El
Lisitskii and N. A. Ladovskii, Moscow 1926; the cover is
reproduced in Sophie Lissitzky-Küppers, *El Lissitzky, Life,
Letters, Texts,* transl. from German by Helene Aldwinckle and
Mary Whittall, London 1980, fig.135.

42 Statement from *ASNOVA* is cited in English in Khan-
Magomedov 1987 (see note 1), p.593; statement from *SA*,
Nos.4-5, 1927, Khan-Magomedov, p.595.

43 *Arkhitektura: raboty Arkhitekturnogo fakul'teta Vkhutemasa,*
Moscow: Izdanie Vkhutemasa, 1927 (Sept) (C.190.aaa.25).

44 V. Lavrov, 'Arkhitektura Vkhutemasa', *Stroitel'stvo Moskvy*,
No.11, 1927, Moscow: pp.15-17. *Stroitel'stvo Moskvy*, Moscow:
Moskovskii Sovet Rabochikh Deputatov, 1927-40, British
Library holdings: 1927: Nos.2-4, 7-12; 1928: Nos.1-6, 9; 1929,
No.10; 1935: Nos.2/3, 13/14, 15, 17/18; 1936: Nos.1-5, 7-13/14,
17, 21, 23-24; 1937: Nos.1-23/24; 1938: Nos.5, 20; 1939: Nos.
1-23/24; 1940: Nos.1-10, 15, 16, 18-20, 23-24 (PP.8006.uw).

45 Resolution of the Moscow City Duma, 16 June 1915, *Izvestiia
Moskovskoi gorodskoi dumy,* Vol.xli, No.2, Feb. 1917, p.59: see

S. Frederick Starr, *Melnikov, Solo Architect in a Mass Society*, New Jersey, Princeton, 1981, p.133.

46 *XIV s''ezd Vsesoiuznoi kommunisticheskoi partii (b)*, Moscow: 1926, pp.737-8, cited in Starr 1981 (see previous note), p.133.

47 Starr 1981 (see note 45), p.134.

48 Mel'nikov's designs and photographs of the finished building taken at the time are reproduced in Starr 1981 (see note 45), pp.134-9. A recent view of the street façade is reproduced in Kopp 1985 (see note 26), p.140.

49 The difference of approach between Rationalists and Constructivists is discussed in Kopp 1985 (see note 26), chapter VI, pp.124-40.

50 Khan-Magomedov 1987 (see note 1 above), p.344.

51 'Excerpts from the works of A. M. Kollontay – Women's Labour in Economic Development, 1923', *Changing Attitudes in Soviet Russia. The Family in the USSR: Documents and Readings*, ed. by Rudolf Schlesinger, London 1949, p.58.

52 *SA*, No.3, 1930, p.15.

53 *SA*, No.1/2, 1930, cited in English in Kopp 1985 (see note 26), p.147.

54 A. Pasternak, 'Spory o budushchem gorode', *SA*, No.1/2, 1930, pp.60, 62, cited in English in Kopp 1985, as previous note.

55 *Stroitel'stvo Moskvy*, No.5, 1930, pp.450 ff., cited in English in Starr 1981 (see note 45), p.170. (This issue of *Stroitel'stvo Moskvy* is not in the collection of the British Library.)

56 *SA*, No.1/2, 1930. English translation from Kopp 1985 (see note 26), p.150.

57 Reproduced in Kopp 1985 (see note 26), p.148, *SA*, No.1/2, 1930.

58 Kopp 1985 (see note 26), p.156, citation with no page number, from 'Memories of a German Communist on his return from the USSR bringing with him the observations of a Soviet bureaucrat', quoted in Kopp from P. Broué, *Le parti bolchevik*, Paris 1963 (no page reference given).

59 *Arkhitektura SSSR: organ Soiuza sovetskikh arkhitektorov*, Moscow 1933-. British Library holdings: 1933: Nos.1,2; 1934: Nos.1-12; 1935: Nos.1-12; 1936- (PP.1667.h).

60 *Arkhitektura SSSR*, No.9, 1934, p.43, cited in English in Starr 1981 (see note 45), p.188.

61 See *Problems of Soviet Literature*, ed. by H. G. Scott, London 1935, reprinted as *Soviet Writers' Congress, 1934: The Debate on Socialist Realism and Modernism in the Soviet Union*, London 1977.

62 The architects' conference was held in November, see 'Sovetskie arkhitektory gotoviatsia k s''ezdu', *Arkhitektura SSSR*, No.10, 1934, p.1.

63 Soiuz sovetskikh arkhitektorov, *Pervoe vsesoiuznoe soveshchanie sovetskikh arkhitektorov: informatsionnyi biulleten'*, No.2, Moscow 1934, p.16 cited in Starr 1981 (see note 45), p.215.

64 Starr points out that delegates of the Proletarian Architects from Armenia and Georgia made the bitterest criticisms; Starr 1981 (see previous note), pp.215-6; his source is as previous note, p.16.

65 Iofan's design is discussed in *Arkhitektura SSSR*, No.2, 1934.

66 See, for example, a reproduction of a prison perspective by Piranesi in *Stroitel'stvo Moskvy*, No.4, 1935, p.35.

67 Ia. Chernikhov, *Osnovy sovremennoi arkhitektury: eksperimental'no-issledovatel'skie raboty*, Leningrad: Izdanie Leningradskogo obshchestva arkhitektorov (LAO), Leningrad, 1930; republished late 1931 with an extra preface in back of book (C.185.bb.7). A 1931 edition with a different cover design is reproduced in Catherine Cooke, *Chernikhov Fantasy and Construction, Iakov Chernikhov's approach to architectural design*, Architectural Design Profile, ed. by Andreas Papadakis, London 1984, p.4.

68 Chernikhov's book was reviewed inside the back cover of *SA*, No.3, 1930.

69 Ia. Chernikhov, *Ornament: kompozitsionno-klassicheskie postroeniia*, Leningrad: published by the author, 1931 (C.185.bb.10).

70 Ia. Chernikhov, *Konstruktsiia arkhitekturnykh i mashinykh form*, Leningrad: Izdanie Leningradskogo obshchestva arkhitektorov, 1931 (C.185.bb.4). English transl. in Cooke 1984 (see note 67), pp.41-80.

71 Ia. Chernikhov with D. Kopanitsyn and E. Pavlova, *Arkhitekturnye fantazii: 101 kompozitsiia v kraskakh; 101 arkhitekturnaia miniatiura*, Leningrad, Izdanie Leningradskogo oblastnogo otdeleniia Vsesoiuznogo ob''edineniia 'Mezhdunarodnaia kniga', 1933 (C.185.bb.5).

72 El Lissitzky, *Russland, die Rekonstruktion der Architektur in der Sowjetunion*, (Neues Bauen in der Welt, Vol.1) Vienna 1930 (Cup.410.g.7). English translation: El Lissitzky, *Russia: An Architecture for World Revolution*, transl. by Eric Dlhosch, London 1970; this is not a facsimile; the original plates are reproduced but with different numbering.

73 Assotsiatsiia khudozhnikov revoliutsionnoi Rossii, abbreviated to AKhRR. Elizabeth Valkenier gives an account of both groups in her *Russian Realist Art, The State and Society: The Peredvizhniki and Their Tradition*, Ann Arbor 1977, pp.149-59.

74 N. Punin, *Noveishie techeniia v russkom iskusstve*, 2 vols, Leningrad: Izdanie Gosudarstvennogo Russkogo Museia, 1927, 1928 (Cup.408.d.23).

75 *Iskusstvo rabochikh: kruzhki IZO rabochikh klubov Leningrada i masterskie IZO Oblpolitprosveta pri DPR im. Gertsena*, exhibition catalogue, Leningrad: Izdanie Gosudarstvennogo Russkogo Muzeia, 1928 (August) (Cup.408.d.31).

76 Ia. Tugendkhol'd, *Iskusstvo oktiabr'skoi epokhi*. Preface by D. Arkin. Leningrad: Academia, 1930 (Cup.408.z.4).

77 O. M. Beskin, *Formalizm v zhivopisi*, Moscow: Vserossiiskii kooperativnyi soiuz rabotnikov izobrazitel'nykh iskusstv, 1933 (X.410/5696).

78 A retrospective exhibition of the work of Pavel Filonov was hung at the Russian Museum in Leningrad in 1929 but his work was already so controversial that the original catalogue introduction by Vera Anikeva was not printed and a second one, critical of the work, substituted. The show never opened, thus denying a most original artist a retrospective in his lifetime. Anikeva's introduction is published in French translation in Troels Andersen and Ksenia Grigorieva, *Art et poésie russes 1900-1930, textes choisis*, ed. by Olga Makhroff and Stanislas Zadora, Paris 1979, pp.254-71.

79 As well as the numerous books on aspects of avant-garde Russian art that were published in the West, Anatole Kopp reminds us that in the 1960s Soviet 1920s architecture and town planning suddenly became so fashionable that various European architecture schools produced 'so-called "Constructivist" and "Rationalist" projects, "references" were evident in buildings' and in some cases the journal *SA* 'replaced the complete works of Le Corbusier and those of the Bauhaus as the preferred stylistic source', Kopp 1985 (see note 26), p.6.

'MAF'
Moscow Association of
Futurists, imprint
designed at *VKhUTEMAS*,
in N. Aseev, *Steel
Nightingale*, 1922
(C.108.bb.44).

Select bibliography

Andersen, Troels, and Ksenia Grigorieva, *Art et poésie russes 1900-1930: textes choisis*, ed. by Olga Makhroff and Stanislas Zadora, Paris 1979

Tradition and Revolution: The Jewish Renaissance in Russian Avant-Garde Art 1912-1928, ed. by Ruth Apter-Gabriel, exhibition catalogue, The Israel Museum, Jerusalem 1987

Art into Life: Russian Constructivism 1914-1932, exhibition catalogue [Henry Art Gallery of the University of Washington, Seattle/Walker Art Center, Minneapolis], New York 1990

Bann, Stephen, ed., *The Tradition of Constructivism*, New York 1974

Bird, Alan, *A History of Russian Painting*, Oxford 1987

Bowlt, John E., ed., *Russian Art of the Avant Garde: Theory and Criticism 1902-1934*, New York 1976 and (revised edition) London 1988

Braun, Edward, *Meyerhold on Theatre*, London 1969

Brown, Edward J., *The Proletarian Episode in Russian Literature, 1928-1932*, New York 1953

Cooke, Catherine, ed., *Russian Avant-Garde Art and Architecture* (Architectural Design Profile, Vol.53,516), London and New York 1983

Fauchereau, Serge, ed., *Moscow 1900-1930*, New York 1988

Fitzpatrick, Sheila, *The Commissariat of Enlightenment: Soviet Organisation of Education and the Arts under Lunacharsky, October 1917-21*, Cambridge 1970

Freeman, Joseph, Joshua Kunitz, Louis Lozowick, *Voices of October: Art and Literature in Soviet Russia*, New York 1930

Hayward, Max, and Labedz, Leopold, eds, *Literature and Revolution in Soviet Russia 1917-1962*, London 1963

Iliazd, exhibition catalogue, Centre Georges Pompidou, Paris 1978

Janecek, Gerald, *The Look of Russian Literature: Avant-Garde Visual Experiments, 1900-1930*, New Jersey 1984

Jangfeldt, Bengt, *Majakovskij and Futurism 1917-1921*, Stockholm 1977

Kasack, Wolfgang, *Dictionary of Russian Literature since 1917*, transl. from German by Maria Carlson and Jane T. Hedges; bibliographical revision by Rebecca Atack, New York 1988

Khan-Magomedov, Selim O., *Rodchenko: The Complete Works*, ed. by Vieri Quilici, transl. from Italian by Huw Evans, London 1986

Khan-Magomedov, Selim O., *Pioneers of Soviet Architecture: The Search for New Solutions in the 1920s and 1930s*, transl. from Russian by Alexander Lieven, ed. by Catherine Cooke, London 1987

Lavrentiev, Alexander, *Varvara Stepanova: A Constructivist Life*, transl. from Russian by Wendy Salmond, ed. by John E. Bowlt, London 1988

Lavrent'ev, Aleksandr, *A. M. Rodchenko, V. F. Stepanova (Mastera sovetskogo knizhnogo iskusstva)* Moscow 1989

Lissitzky-Küppers, Sophie, *El Lissitzky, Life, Letters, Texts*, transl. from German by Helen Aldwinckle and Mary Whittall, London 1980

Leclanche-Boulé, Claude, *Typographies et photomontages constructivistes en URSS*, Paris 1984

Leyda, Jay, *Kino: A History of Russian and Soviet Film*, London 1960

Lodder, Christina, *Russian Constructivism*, New Haven and London 1983

Markov, Vladimir, *Russian Futurism: A History*, London 1969

Mason, Rainer Michael, *Moderne. Postmoderne, deux cas d'école, l'avant-garde russe et hongroise 1916-1925, Giorgio de Chirico 1924-1934*, Geneva 1988

Nisbet, Peter, *El Lissitzky 1890-1941*, exhibition catalogue, Harvard University Art Museums, Cambridge Mass. 1987

Oliva, Achille Bonito, *La parola totale: una tradizione futurista 1909-1986*, exhibition catalogue, Galleria Fonte d'Abisso, Modena 1986

Paris-Moscou, exhibition catalogue, Musée nationale d'art moderne, Centre Georges Pompidou, Paris 1978

Passuth, Krisztina, *Les avant-gardes de l'Europe centrale, 1907-1927*, Paris 1988

Roman, Gail Harrison, *Ex Libris 6: Constructivism and Futurism: Russian and Other*, New York 1977

Rudnitsky, Konstantin, *Russian and Soviet Theatre: Tradition and the Avant-Garde*, transl. from Russian by Roxane Permar, ed. by Lesley Milne, London 1988

Soviet Writers' Congress, 1934: The Debate on Socialist Realism and Modernism in the Soviet Union, London 1977

Stupples, Peter, *Pavel Kuznetsov: his Life and Art*, Cambridge 1989

Taylor, Brandon, *Art and Literature under the Bolsheviks. Vol.1: The Crisis of Renewal 1917-1924*, London/Concord, Mass. 1991

Terras, Victor, ed., *Handbook of Russian Literature*, New Haven/London 1985

Valkenier, Elizabeth, *Russian Realist Art, The State and Society: The Peredvizhniki and Their Tradition*, Ann Arbor 1977

Zavalishin, V., *Early Soviet Writers*, New York 1958

Kirill Zdanevich and Cubo-Futurism, Tiflis 1918-1920, exhibition catalogue, Rachel Adler Gallery, New York 1987

Zhadova, Larissa A., *Malevich: Suprematism and Revolution in Russian Art 1910-1930*, London 1978

Zhadova, Larissa, ed., *Tatlin*, London 1988

Index of illustrations

Numbers refer to pages on which black and white illustrations are
shown; colour plate numbers are in bold, with page references.

Index

V. Mayakovsky

монтаж варвары степановой
фото б. игнатэвич